Jabez Lamar Monroe Curry

Constitutional Government in Spain

Jabez Lamar Monroe Curry

Constitutional Government in Spain

ISBN/EAN: 9783337230289

Printed in Europe, USA, Canada, Australia, Japan

Cover: Foto ©Suzi / pixelio.de

More available books at **www.hansebooks.com**

Constitutional Government in Spain

A Sketch

BY

J. L. M. CURRY, LL.D.
LATE MINISTER OF THE UNITED STATES IN SPAIN

NEW YORK
HARPER & BROTHERS, FRANKLIN SQUARE
1889

LOVINGLY

I Dedicate this Little Volume

TO

MARY WORTHAM THOMAS CURRY

On the twenty-first anniversary of our marriage. For whatever I may have accomplished during this nearly quarter of a century, for any success in my mission at Madrid, I am very largely indebted to her unwearied patience, to her wise and thoughtful helpfulness.

PREFACE.

A STUDY of Spain, her manners, politics, institutions, and people, was a necessary part of my duties while residing in Madrid. What interested me may give some pleasure to such of my countrymen as may honor this little book with a perusal. American writers have done much to familiarize intelligent persons with the romance, the history, the literature, the art, the scenery of Spain. I have sought rather to trace the history of an idea, and to help the student of the science of government. Only so much of history has been given as was thought essential to a better understanding of the progress of constitutional and free government.

J. L. M. C.

CONTENTS.

CHAPTER I.
Evolution of Constitutional Government Slow. — Experiments Tentative.—The Sketch helpful in Appreciating and Guarding our Republic.—Comparative Politics.—A Little History to link Transition Periods.............*Page* 1

CHAPTER II.
The Constitution of 1812.—Some of its Features.—Struggle for Existence.—The Constitution of 1837............ 6

CHAPTER III.
Accession of Isabella.—Troublous Condition of the Country.—Constitution of 1845.—Insurrections.—Flight of Isabella.—Constitution of 1869.—Great Advance in Political Ideas.—Religious Freedom........................ 17

CHAPTER IV.
Choice of a King.—Candidates and the Elected.—Effect of calling Leopold to the Throne.—Franco-Prussian War.—Election of Amadeo.—Subsequent Abdication........ 31

CHAPTER V.
Difficulties of the Situation.—Establishment of the Republic.—Recognition by the United States................ 47

CHAPTER VI.
Presidents and Policy.—Overthrow of the Republic.—Rapid Changes..................................... 58

CHAPTER VII.
Causes of the Fall.—Account of the Presidents.—Abrupt Transition.—The Army.—False Hopes.—Madrid.. *Page* 66

CHAPTER VIII.
Pronunciamento for Alfonso........................ 84

CHAPTER IX.
Constitution of 1876.—Freedom of Worship in Spain.... 88

CHAPTER X.
Cabinet Government............................... 96

CHAPTER XI.
Progress of Liberal Institutions in Spain.—Platform of Liberal and Conservative Parties..................... 100

CHAPTER XII.
Policy of the Republican Party.................... 114

CHAPTER XIII.
Reforms Needed.—Hope for the Future.............. 127

APPENDIX A.
Sketches of Fernando, Leopold, Duke of Montpensier, and Amadeo.. 135

APPENDIX B.
Sketches of Christina, Isabel, Alfonso XII., the Infantas, the Queen-regent, and Alfonso XIII................... 150

APPENDIX C.
Present Aspect of Spain........................... 170

APPENDIX D.
The Acquisition of Florida........................ 186

A SKETCH
OF
CONSTITUTIONAL GOVERNMENT
IN SPAIN
AND OF
THE REPUBLIC.

CHAPTER I.

Evolution of Constitutional Government Slow. — Experiments Tentative.—The Sketch helpful in Appreciating and Guarding our Republic.—Comparative Politics.—A Little History to link Transition Periods.

In this sketch, Constitution is not used in a vague or general sense, but as embodying, in written form or exact definition, the organic law of the State as contradistinguished from prescription, statutes, or royal decrees.

The history of the establishment and growth of a constitutional government is not the recital of a naked abstraction, but an account of human progress with the favoring or hindering motives which spring from the nobler or the meaner nature of man. Such a government is no sudden creation nor easy achievement. It costs experiments, failures, sacrifices, revolutions, wars. The people fail to realize how reluctantly privilege relaxes its grasp, or traditional wrongs and usurpations yield to the demands for liberty, equality, and fraternity. The excesses of the French Revolution, so commonly used to point censures of popular rule, had their occasion in the violence of popular passion, but their cause was in the tyrannies and corruptions of government and aristocracy and Church. The most harmful and indefensible of all usurpations, a State religion, contests every inch in the struggle for freedom and conscience, and rallies and conquers even when the victory seemed to have been won by the Opposition. A debate in the House of Commons in 1886 on disestablishment in Wales, conducted with zeal and ability, presented the singular spectacle of an entire ignoring of the real question. The unanswerable argument, as drawn from the teachings of Christ, from inalienable natural right, from freedom of worship, from individuality of religious duties, from the illegitimacy and tyranny of governmental interference with what pertains exclusively to personal judgment, was not enforced and was scarcely alluded to. So in Spain the battle for constitutional government has been waged for eighty years in the face of the most formidable odds and the most persistent and virulent antagonism. In this period there has been a litter of constitutions: that of the Cortes of Cadiz of 1812; that of Christina of 1836; that of Isabel of 1837; another of Isabel of 1845; that of Prim and others in 1869; that of 1873, and finally that of 1876. New constitutions have superseded the older, to be in turn disregarded or overthrown by the favorite of the hour. It has been too often true that a body without delegated authority therefor has made a constitution which has been suspended or violated at an early day, and the government has been arbitrarily administered in utter disregard of grants and limitations. The history of these tentative and ephemeral constitutions, superficially considered, is adapted to provoke ridicule, but a closer examination will discover an undercurrent moving onward, with many eddies and obstructions, towards a freer government and a better definition and a more stable guaranty of popular rights. A sketch of some of the constitutions and of the Republic, with some details connected with their genesis and workings, may serve to make us more charitable towards those who, in the face of almost insurmountable obstacles, have been striving to imitate our example and secure for their unhappy country the rights and liberties which have made ours so great and prosperous.

If history be philosophy teaching by example, an acquaintance with the experience of fellow-men, closely allied to us by many ties, in their oft-baffled struggles to throw off oppression and attain national and personal freedom, should awaken within us deeper gratitude for what we enjoy and more constant vigilance against the ever-recurring tendencies to injustice and wrong. For the elucidation of constitutional and political progress it has been found necessary to give the contemporaneous history. Perhaps too much has been given, but it has not been easy to resist the temptation to give more when one is writing of a country where truth outruns fiction. The history of a people and the government of a people are too inseparably allied to be understood apart. Stubb's "Select Charters," illustrating both English and American constitutional history, has aided students in the study of comparative constitutions. What Spain has done in civil polity in this century is valuable in itself, and relatively as showing development in government and throwing light on political science. Historical facts are introduced, therefore, to make the discussions more real and concrete. One wishes to see how people have grown, how things have been brought about, and what forces, at different periods in the same country, have been successful in the struggle for personal and constitutional liberty.

CHAPTER II.

The Constitution of 1812.—Some of its Features.—Struggle for Existence.—The Constitution of 1837.

The Peninsular wars, growing out of the restless ambition of Napoleon and the weakness of Charles IV., threw Spain into anarchy. Charles abdicated and abandoned the country. Ferdinand VII. was called to the throne in 1808, the same year in which Joseph Bonaparte,* as a part of the policy to

---

* Dr. Lieber, who knew and corresponded with Joseph Bonaparte when he lived at Bordentown, New Jersey, says he was an affable and lovable man, kind and gentle, and fond of relating occurrences connected with his checkered life. In the Life and Letters of Lieber is published a letter of the ex-king, July 1, 1829, giving an ingenious defence of Napoleonism. As a justification of his brother's singular method of securing "constitutionalism" and "universal equality," Joseph wrote: "The English Cabinet, in rekindling the war, made the continuance of this *despotism* a necessity, for Napoleon was forced to use every means of reconciling the governments of Continental Europe with France. Everything that Napoleon did—his establishment of an unfeudal nobility, his family relations, his Legion of Honor, his new kingdoms—everything was forced upon him. The English obliged him

create a Napoleonic dynasty, was proclaimed king. Overawed and deceived by Napoleon, Ferdinand also soon deserted Spain. By these compulsory abdications, extorted at Bayonne, Spain was left without legitimate authority. Local and general juntas were irregularly appointed, but they failed to command the confidence of the Spaniards or secure the advantage of union. To redress grievances and provide for the public defence, a Cortes was summoned and met September, 1810, at Cadiz, almost the only town in the territory unoccupied by foreign soldiers. Its composition was very popular, but it was not a revolutionary body. The usual civil power having been dispersed or destroyed by conquest, the Cortes was convened to give a regular government and maintain national independence. As a permanent power of nationality, it undertook the public defence, continued the war against the French, made provision for the absence of the executive head, took away the prerogatives of the Crown, and converted absolutism into a con-

---

to do everything that he did by compelling him to put himself into apparent harmony with the nations he had conquered and wished to secure against the fascinations of England."

stitutional government. In 1812 this extraordinary Cortes promulgated a constitution, which was received as the fundamental law wherever the French arms did not stifle the public will. It was the first of a series in the long struggle to overthrow kingly misrule, and to define the rights and liberties of the Spanish people. The bold and hazardous step, a justifiable protest against Bourbonism, was in imitation of American example. It declares that "the sovereignty resides essentially in the nation; and for the same reason, the right of establishing the fundamental laws belongs exclusively to the nation." Misled by the sophisms which misled Franklin, and which control the opinions of some Spanish and English and French radicals of the present day, who advocate the effacement of a second body, the makers of the Constitution provided for only one legislative assembly. Castelar, in 1873, said of the instrument that "it formed the democratic monarchy;" in other words, it subordinated the throne to the law, and partially reasserted the truth embodied in our Declaration of Independence, that governments derive their just powers from the consent of the governed.

This constitution was overthrown by Ferdinand at his restoration in 1814. It was thrust aside by royal usurpation, backed by military force, without a pretext of legal or civil forms. In 1820 it was restored by the army assembled at Cadiz to be embarked against the revolted American colonies. The people sustained the action of the soldiers, and the King even gave his assent.

This first essay at formulating an organic law, and introducing the popular will as a substantive factor in the government of Spain, deserves a fuller consideration. The articles of the Constitution are distributed under ten heads, treating of the nation, the territory, the people, the King, religion, the tribunals of justice, the interior government of towns and provinces, the taxes, public instruction, the army, etc. The article on the organization and attributes of the Cortes declares that the sovereignty resides essentially in the nation, and to it belongs exclusively the right to establish fundamental laws, and to adopt the form of government which may be most expedient. The functions of executive power were distributed into seven departments or ministries, and this was the origin of parliamentary government in Spain; but a further account will be given more conveniently when the Constitution of 1876 is considered. The judicial department was defined and its duties mapped out. The government of the towns was intrusted to the inhabitants, and that of the provinces to provincial deputations. The deputies exercising this local control are chosen for four years under certain restrictions, and are presided over by the Governor. This officer, while looking after the interests of the province, represents at the same time the views of the Government at Madrid which appoints him, and in all elections uses his influence openly and without much scruple in behalf of the ministerial candidates. The deputation is the organ of the wishes and needs of the province, and its sphere of duties embraces moral and material interests, the construction of public works, the establishment of schools, charitable institutions, etc. The Constitution enunciated general principles in reference to the right of petition and freedom of the press, and declared all taxes illegal unless ordered by the Cortes. To prevent encroachments during the vacation, the action of the executive power was to be called in question and rigidly examined at the beginning of each session.

Provision was made for the introduction of trial by jury in case it should be deemed advisable; but this feature of English and American jurisprudence, although partially recognized in the Constitution of 1837, has not yet been incorporated into Spanish law. The Constitution had a preliminary discourse, and was marred by minute details and other defects. It was framed under most adverse circumstances. Ferdinand was in captivity. Contemporaneous with this effort for political regeneration was the terrible struggle for national independence and national existence. The patriotism, sagacity, ability, and courage of the Constitutionalist leaders were confronted by centuries of ignorance, absolutism, and repression of thought. They deserve the gratitude of Spain and the homage of all lovers of constitutional government. The battle for freedom is often baffled. Ferdinand, "although he had committed himself to the Constitution by every variety of gratuitous and supererogatory perjury," eagerly violated his oaths, and used all his power and influence to crush the spirit of the people.

At the Congress of Aix-la-Chapelle, October, 1818, at which Austria, Russia, Great Britain, France, and Spain were represented, projects were entertained of engaging the European Alliance in actual military operations against the South Americans, and a plan for restoring to Spanish authority the Colonies, warring for their independence, was matured; but it failed because Great Britain refused to accede to the condition of employing *force* for its accomplishment. "The Powers," as the sovereigns called themselves in assuming the guardianship of Europe, treated the restoration of the Spanish Constitution as a crime demanding their intervention, and, as Nesselrode declared, "the example of an expiatory act to the people of the two hemispheres," notwithstanding Russia, by solemn treaty, had previously acknowledged "the legitimacy of the general and extraordinary assembly of the Cortes held at Cadiz, as well as the Constitution which they have decreed and sanctioned." Assembled at Troppau in 1820, these sovereigns included the Spanish revolution among the objects of their condemnation, although an eminent English contemporary statesman said that there never was an extensive political change attended with less violence or bloodshed. This Holy Alliance, professing to act in the name and under the protection of Father, Son, and Holy Ghost, asserted its right to interfere in every case where new institutions were established not consistent with "the monarchical principle, which recognizes no institution as legitimate that does not flow spontaneously from the monarch." This was tantamount to an alliance in defence of the hereditary houses of Europe, and against the right of a people to the best possible administration of their affairs. In 1822, with the express sanction and approbation of the other States, and in furtherance and execution of the system which the potentates at Troppau had jointly announced as the rule of their conduct, and to put a stop to what they termed " moral contagion," and to arrest the demoralizing influence of " a national assembly which ventured to think for itself and consult the interests of its country," France invaded Spain, and by armed intervention put down the Constitution of

1812.* This forcible repression at the bidding of the Holy Alliance, invited by Ferdinand and the Spanish aristocracy, illustrated the adage of the return of curses. Canning's South American policy was England's response to this French invasion. He rested his recognition of the South American republics on the unjustifiable pretensions of Spain and the selfish ingratitude of her rulers. When France, by virtue of the decree of the Duke of Angoulême, signed at Andujar August 8, 1823, assumed superiority over all Spanish authorities, and threw an army of one hundred thousand men into the country to control her domestic politics and establish the Bourbon king, England sought to checkmate the movement by recognizing the independence of Mexico, Columbia, and Buenos Ayres; and Canning, in language which has become classic in diplomacy, uttered the boast, " I called the New World into existence to redress the balance of the Old."

With the death of Ferdinand, October 2, 1833, the traditional monarchy may be said

---

* *Edinburgh Review*, vols. xxxviii. and xl.; Circulars of Allied Powers, 1820 and 1821; Annual Register, 1809; and Schoell, 120, 543.

to have fallen. His widow, Christina, became regent, and, to save the throne for her daughter, Isabel II., against the claims and machinations of Don Carlos and the reactionary politicians, she reluctantly allied herself with the Liberal party. As the result of this association, a kind of codification by a royal statute was made, which is often cited as a constitution; but its creation of a chamber of aristocratic peers and a chamber of *procuradores*, to be selected mainly by the corporations of cities and towns, was regarded as a mockery of representation, furnishing no adequate security against misrule and oppression. Mariana, the historian, contemptuously dismisses it: "No limit of sovereign power is sought in it, no guaranty of individual liberty, nothing relative to the judicial order."

In 1836 the soldiers compelled Christina to sign a paper recognizing the Constitution of 1812, and she afterwards proclaimed it, giving to Spaniards an additional reason for heeding the injunction not to put trust in princes. This was but preliminary to a meeting of the Constituent Cortes in 1837, which adopted another organic law that had the prospect of permanency in the fact that it had the sanction of the *Moderados* and *Progresistas,* the two divisions of the Liberal party.

The Constitution of 1837 was less democratic than its predecessor, and therefore, in the opinion of the nobility, better adapted to the capabilities of the people and the interests of the nation. It did not depart from the principle that the people were the ultimate source of all political power, and it retained the responsibility of the Ministry. It differed from the Constitution of 1812 in having two co-legislative bodies of senators and deputies, the members of each chamber having a different mode of selection or constituency, thus preserving the advantage of concurrence and of a check on hasty or unwise legislation. Suffrage was restricted, and in the Crown was lodged an absolute veto.

CHAPTER III.

Accession of Isabella.—Troublous Condition of the Country.—Constitution of 1845.—Insurrections.—Flight of Isabella.—Constitution of 1869.—Great Advance in Political Ideas.—Religious Freedom.

On the death of Ferdinand, and during the minority of Isabella II., the wicked Christina became regent. In consequence of a popular outbreak, she renounced, in 1840, the regency, and retired to France. At that time the Government was Liberal, drawing its power in part from the popular will, but chiefly from the military influence of its head, General Espartero, in whose honor as a pacificator an equestrian statue was erected, in 1887, in Madrid. The question of a regent excited much discussion and dissension, whether there should be one or three, and who should be chosen. The Cortes, in joint meeting in the Hall of the Senate, by a vote of 153 to 136 decided on a single regent, and by ballot elected Espartero, giving him 179 votes. On May 10th he took the prescribed oaths and presented himself before the Queen at the palace. It has been noted as the first instance of the kind in a monarchical government that when the Queen in person, in December, opened the Cortes, the regent read, in her name, a speech which departed from the custom of stating only vague generalities. Years of civil war were necessary to decide the succession between Don Carlos, the brother, and Isabel, the daughter, of Ferdinand. The unhappy and disastrous reign of the Queen was a poor compensation for all it cost to seat her upon the throne. The memory of that dreadful conflict and the vicissitudes through which the country passed seem to justify the remark made in 1842 by Washington Irving, our Minister, that " Spain is a country accustomed to violent remedies, and seems now and then to require a political Sangrado." The turbulent population was instigated to frequent outbreaks and insurrections. The Government, like some mysterious persons in every community, had an inscrutable secret of subsisting without visible means, for resources were anticipated, and the treasury was habitually empty. The licentiousness of the press had no bounds. Patriotic feeling was lost in the violence of factions. Sedition was fed by the lavish distribution of money. An attempt at the abduction of the Queen came nigh being successful. Ministries were fickle and fleeting. The capital was besieged. A revolutionary government was established. Espartero fled, and the idol became an exile. On November 8, 1843, the Queen at thirteen was declared of age, and was sworn in as reigning sovereign, notwithstanding the Constitution fixed fourteen years as the term of the royal majority. The doubtful expedient brought no calm to the perturbed country. Discord soon appeared in the palace and spread into the streets. Rejoicings at the accession were soon followed by factious clamors and angry tumults, and by conspiracies to bring a constitutional monarchy into disrepute, and restore absolutism. The Queen became an object of party odium, was charged with deceit and falsehood, and with being a mere manikin in the hands of designing courtiers.

These complications and disorders, and others of equal seriousness, were not favorable to improved government, but the Cortes, under the influence of Narvaez, and sheltered by the principle of the omnipotence of Parliament, and without special authorization, undertook to reform the Constitution of 1837. At the close of the Cortes, on May 22, 1845, the Queen, in person, promulgated the reformed constitution. Washington Irving makes this comment: "Scoffed at by Absolutists and Progresistas, it is an instrument which gives satisfaction to no one, for its very devisers consider it a compromise between their consciences and interests, with which they vainly hope to beguile the people. I have forborne of late to attempt to trace the tortuous course of Spanish politics, where everything is perplexed with mystery and intrigue, where even those in power who have good intentions find themselves overreached or undermined by adverse influences." A very able American lawyer has remarked of this instrument that it did not surround the exercise of absolute dominion by the powers that be with any insurmountable barriers. To almost every right secured to the citizen there is attached a significant clause, which has the real effect of setting the whole matter at sea. For instance, a Spaniard may print and publish his ideas freely, *but with subjection to the laws.* So as to right of petition, asylum of domicile, personal liberty, etc. The protection is dependent on the temper of the law-making department. By this constitution, which has no jury clause, as had those of 1812 and 1837, the senators were nominated by the Crown for life, and were to be taken from certain functionaries or grandees enjoying a fixed income from land or other stable sources. In 1857 it was provided that the dignity of senators should be hereditary in the families of grandees, upon condition of the requisite income; and to secure this property qualification the entail of estates was permitted. In 1864 a new ministry succeeded in carrying a law by which, in principle, the hereditary right of grandees to have, under certain conditions, a seat in the Senate was abolished, and thus re-established, in this particular, the Constitution of 1845.

In January, 1866, occurred an insurrection headed by General Prim, a leading officer of the army, which, failing, caused his temporary exile. In June there originated in the barrack of San Gil, a few hundred yards from the palace, a more serious revolt, which extended over a great part of Madrid. In October of the same year the Ministry, in a public proclamation, alleged as a justification for an autocratic exercise of power, that " revolutionary tendencies constituted an imposing organism with dangerous pretensions; that a rebellion adverse to the fundamental institutions of the country and the dynasty of Isabella, such as had never been seen in Spain, had obtained possession of important municipalities, and triumphed in the deputations from all the provinces," and that it was necessary to dissolve the municipalities and renew the provincial deputations. As these " reforms" could not be effected without " restoring the systematic fitness of different points of law," the Government, by a decree " under the royal rubric," abrogated the laws on the organization and administration of the municipalities and the provinces " until the approbation of the Cortes should be obtained." By this arbitrary assumption Spain was under as complete a despotism as existed in the neighboring empire of Morocco. The dissatisfaction at such maladministration, such abuses in the government, and the thinly disguised immoralities of the Queen, soon found expression in audible murmurs and severe criticism. These verbal protests were followed by machinations for the overthrow or control of a sovereign subject to ambitious priests and a venal coterie. Two exiles, Marshal Serrano and Marshal Prim, united with Admiral Topete at Cadiz, and began a revolution which soon had the sympathy and co-operation of a large part of the army and the navy. A provisional revolutionary junta of forty-one persons — a few others, notably Sagasta and Martos, were afterwards added — was appointed, which signed decrees and orders having the force and effect of laws. In less than a month Francisco Serrano was authorized by the junta to form a temporary ministry to rule the country until the Cortes should meet.

The defeat of the royal troops near Alcolea prevented the return of Isabella to Madrid, and on September 30, 1868, she fled across the border into France. Driven from power and exiled, almost without resistance, remonstrance, or regret, the fall of the Bourbons finds its only parallel in Spanish history in the suddenness and indifference with which the subsequent dynasty of Amadeo disappeared. With the flight of the Queen vanished for a time the parliamentary monarchy, and, despite her impotent proclamations from France, and offers of amnesty, a provisional government was at once established.

A decree of the Government to take inventories of all the libraries, collections of manuscripts, works of art, or objects of historical value—a measure necessary to make useful and available these treasures, and to prevent spoliation and transfer—was peacefully executed except at Burgos. Here, under instigation of the priests and aided by them, a mob assembled, broke down the doors of the cathedral, assassinated the Governor, wounded the chief of police, and expelled those engaged in making the required examination and inventory. This outbreak, attributed to a clerical and Carlist conspiracy, awakened opposition and horror. A strong pressure was created for the immediate establishment of freedom of worship. The atrocious butchery at Burgos aroused the inhabitants of the capital. The Nuncio was so imperilled by the excited populace that the diplomatic corps interposed for the safety and protection of their colleague. Marshal Serrano quieted the angry multitude gathered at his residence by saying that the Government had prepared the project of a constitution to be submitted to the Constitutional Assembly, one of whose first articles was liberty of worship.

On February 12, 1869, the Constitutional Cortes, convoked by the Provisional Government, assembled with unusual pomp and ceremony and with striking demonstrations of popular enthusiasm.* The Republican element had many and strong supporters. *Viva la República!* was their deafening shout. *Viva la Monarquia!* was the response of the Opposition. General Serrano, Duke de la Torre, said only one viva should be given, *Viva the Sovereignty of the People.*

---

* On the organization of the Cortes Constituyéntes, General Serrano resigned his power into their hands, but the Cortes passed a vote of thanks, and intrusted him with the formation of a new ministry. He continued the cabinet which four months before he had called around him at the instance of the junta. In it were Prim, Figuerola, Sagasta, Topete, and Zorrilla.

The dethroned queen from France asserted her royal rights, but political parties were numerous. The Republicans, among whom the eloquent Castelar was influential, were a compact phalanx, and to them the independent Progresistas, led by General Prim, made overtures which were accepted. On Sunday, June 5, 1869, the Constitution was promulgated. The whole city came out in gala dress and gave itself up to hilarity and festivity. The palace of the Congress was elaborately ornamented, and a platform extending the whole length of the building was occupied by the diplomatic corps and other distinguished people. The Constitution was read to an immense concourse, estimated at one hundred thousand, and the American Minister, Hon. John P. Hale, said, "Everybody seemed to rejoice at the coming of a new order of things." While recognizing the provinces and endowing them with important functions, the Cortes rejected the plan of a federal republic, and adhered to the monarchical form of government as corresponding with and a concession to Spanish traditions, and as most likely to secure a larger measure of the liberal principles of the revolution. The Constitution, the legitimate outgrowth of that popular uprising, recognized the natural and inherent rights of man, and established an elective monarchy. A monarchy harmonized with the existing governments of Europe, and past bitter experience had shown how readily and effectively they would combine against any political action which did not acknowledge hereditary right and privileged classes as the only proper basis of civil polity. The action of the Holy Alliance at Troppau was a significant and fearful claim of the right of the European powers "to take a hostile attitude in regard to those States in which the overthrow of the Government might operate as an example." Congress was chosen by universal suffrage. The provincial assemblies and the municipal authorities were elected by the people of their respective localities. The ancient privileges of the aristocracy were annulled, and the equality of all men before the law was recognized.

The best test of the growth and establishment of free and enlightened principles of government is the freedom guaranteed to worship and the abstinence of civil discrimination among forms of religious faith. In 1868, General Prim, replying to an inquiry of H. Guedalla, Esq., a Hebrew, said, "I am convinced that the triumph of the revolution must bring about, without any restriction, every religious liberty." The same person having asked a formal authorization for the Jews to enter Spain by means of the revocation of the edict of banishment of March 20, 1492, elicited from the Minister of Grace and Justice a reply that the Provisional Government was prepared to fulfil all the engagements it had contracted respecting other worship different from the Catholic. In 1869 Serrano wrote to Sir Moses Montefiore, the distinguished Hebrew philanthropist, "This government wishes to put on record once more its unalterable determination that the regenerating principle of liberty shall extend its beneficial influence to that which is dearest and most sacred to the human conscience, viz., to Religious Creeds." "No disability weighs in Spain upon the professors of any creed whatsoever. This conduct faithfully reflects the wishes of a country determined to remain no longer stagnant in the midst of the fruitful progress of Europe."

This great change in public opinion, traditions, and law was too much of an advance in freedom not to meet with stubborn and wicked resistance. Accordingly, the Clerical party claimed the continued maintenance of the Roman Catholic Church and the exclusion of all other worship, but the country had outgrown such intolerance. Mr. Hale, with a large generalization from few facts, exultingly wrote that Protestantism had taken a firm hold, and that the Spanish Protestant church in Madrid was crowded every Sunday to overflowing. The Catholic form of faith was retained in the organic law as the religion of the State, but a larger liberty of worship was secured to the people. In Article XXI. the Catholic Apostolic Roman religion was declared the State religion, and the obligation to maintain its worship and ministers was imposed. Foreigners were granted toleration for public and private worship under the limitations of the universal rules of morals and right, and Spaniards, even, professing another than the Catholic religion were to have the like toleration. This progress is the more marked if we remember that Spain is the most intensely

Catholic country in Europe; that by the concordat concluded with Pius IX. in 1851 the Catholic religion was to be maintained as "the exclusive religion of the realm in such sort that the practice of all other worship shall be forbidden and prevented," and that she aligns herself slowly and reluctantly with the modern ideas of soul liberty as formulated in the American constitutions.

Spain quietly passed from the anomalous condition of a provisional into a regular constitutional government, the title of Provisional Government having been changed to that of Executive Power. In June a regency was established, and Serrano was chosen by a vote of 193 to 45. From June 16, 1869, the date of Prim's first cabinet, until December 27, 1870, when he was shot, he had four separate ministries besides several changes of individual ministers; and this instability is characteristic of Spanish politics. In March, 1870, Sigismund Moret, the distinguished orator and Liberal statesman, first appeared in the cabinet, having the portfolio of the Colonies.

CHAPTER IV.

Choice of a King.—Candidates and the Elected.—Effect of calling Leopold to the Throne.—Franco-Prussian War.—Election of Amadeo.—Subsequent Abdication.

Two serious questions confronted the Government and the nation—(1) political, Who shall be king? and (2) financial, How shall the exhausted treasury be replenished and the ever-recurring deficit be met and prevented? Expenditure and receipts would not balance, and the sources of income were deceptive. The difficulties and diversities of opinion attending the choice of a king distracted the Monarchists, and gave increasing vitality and efficiency to the Republican organization, notwithstanding the abdication of the Queen in favor of her son, Alfonso. In October "a federal republican insurrection" occurred at Valencia, and a large force was needed to suppress it. In Tarragona, Barcelona, Saragossa, Seville, and other towns, there was a marked increase of democratic sentiment. To prevent the spread of this feeling, the provisions of the Constitution guaranteeing personal rights were suspended, more than twenty journals were suppressed, and the regular authorities in many municipalities were dismissed. These suspended provisions were afterwards restored, but little was done towards adapting the old laws to the new order. Many of the deputies on the Government side of the chamber held positions which prevented independence in their legislative action, and the people justly complained at their failure to realize the advantages sought and expected from the revolution.

The expediency of having a king being determined on, it was thought necessary that he should be a Roman Catholic, and, under the narrow worship of mere birth, that he should be also of royal blood. Available persons with these requisites were few, and thus the field of selection was very limited. There was not wanting much " electioneering " by candidates or their adherents. The Spanish succession had long been a source of international strife ; and so the question of a sovereign agitated other countries besides Spain, and the solicitude of Spanish statesmen to find a proper solution of this problem had irritation and perplexity from abroad. A crown is such a glittering prize that it tempts human ambition and cupidity. Maximilian is a striking illustration of what men and nations will venture for dynastic strengthening, for national interests, and for individual aggrandizement. It was not strange that other European nations, in the presence of imminent Continental conflicts, should strive, openly or furtively, to gain a willing ally or preponderance of influence in the Peninsula.

For the vacant throne some Spaniards turned to the Duke of Montpensier; some to the Court of Portugal, and in default thereof to the house of Savoy. The Portuguese search originated in the somewhat vague but ever-ardent aspiration for Iberian unity, the secret desire of every Spanish statesman, and had the active co-operation of some influential men who solicited the assent and intervention of Napoleon. The negotiations with Portugal were prosecuted not without difficulty, but also not without some hope of success. Ferdinand, however, declined the proffered crown, and then, at the moment of

3

greatest embarrassment, the candidature of Leopold, Prince of Hohenzollern, was proposed. This was in pursuance of the desire for Peninsular union, and was "a natural consequence of King Ferdinand's refusal to accept the crown of Spain." A distinguished Spaniard, a participant in the events, has kindly furnished this explanation of the action of his government: " Prince Leopold is married to the Infanta Antonia of Portugal, sister of the present monarch, and for this reason his candidacy responded to the aspirations of the Liberal party for Iberian union. It was initiated by the Duke of Saldanha, at that time in Paris, and in concert, according to report, with the Princess Mathilda, cousin of the Emperor. General Prim adopted the suggestion with ardor, and sent a Spanish diplomats, Señor Salazzar y Mazarredo, to Dusseldorf, the residence of the prince and princess, with a letter offering the throne to Prince Leopold. The prince accepted, and his reply was brought to Madrid by Salazzar on the last day of June. By a fatal coincidence, it happened that General Prim, on the day of the arrival, was hunting in the mountains of Toledo. The former, satisfied with his mission, and believing its success assured, prematurely read the letter which he brought to various public men, among them Messrs. Rivero and Zorrilla. The result was that when General Prim arrived that night in Madrid everybody knew what had occurred, and the secrecy indispensable to the success of the negotiation was made impossible."

It was the intention of General Prim, when the acceptance had been once secured, to confer with the Emperor Napoleon, whose acquiescence he considered indispensable to the establishing of the prince in Spain. His plan was to have a conference in person with the Emperor at Vichy, and he was preparing to go to these baths as soon as he had received the answer he was expecting. "The publicity given to the candidacy not only destroyed all this plan, but precipitated the events which afterwards developed, and which, being entirely public, need not be referred to. So impressed was General Prim with the necessity of coming to an understanding with Napoleon in reference to the candidacy for the Spanish throne, if the reply of the Emperor had been negative the candidature would not have been known. If the Emperor had assented, success was beyond a doubt."

"To what point the King of Prussia had knowledge through his representative in Madrid of the plans and intentions of General Prim, is a matter about which nothing is yet known certainly. What is beyond a doubt in the minds of all those who were at the time acquainted with the negotiation is that it was not fostered by the King of Prussia, nor did Bismarck believe that it could be the origin or occasion of a conflict. After war had been declared Napoleon informed Prim that he knew the loyalty of his conduct, and did not hold him responsible for what had occurred."

Early in July, 1870 (the 3d), General Prim announced to the French ambassador the purpose of the Council of Ministers to offer the crown to Leopold. In fact, as has been stated, the offer by a deputation and its acceptance had preceded the annunciation, and the choice and the haste were to defeat the schemes of Montpensier. Prim said to the ambassador that he should have needed to relax his hand only a little and Montpensier would have been chosen. The negotiation and agreement, when they transpired, were regarded by other Powers as an unwise disturbance of the European equilibrium. The *Times* characterized the election as a vulgar and impudent *coup-d'état*. France was indignant, and looked upon it as a dynastic intrigue, and an adroit and Machiavelian scheme on the part of Bismarck to put her between two fires. To place on the Spanish throne a member of the reigning house of Prussia and reunite two thrones in the same dynasty, Duke de Gramont said, was "au profit de la Prusse, un point d'appui contre la France." In the case of war there would be no security for the frontier of the Pyrenees if a Prussian prince occupied the throne of Spain, and an army to guard it would be necessary. A distinguished Spaniard, who knew Eugénie well before her marriage, and preserved relations of close friendship with her when she became empress, says that she was much excited over the intelligence, and declared that his acceptance would be followed by a war with Prussia, and that Spain would suffer sorely from the conflict. France, finding herself in the presence of an act of political aggression, declared that she would never consent to see a Prussian prince seated on the throne of Spain, and explanations were demanded from the Berlin Cabinet. Bismarck alleged that the King of Prussia gave his consent to the acceptance of the crown by the prince only as the head of the Hohenzollern family, and not as an act of the Government. This was a lame explanation, and an effort was made through Benedetti, the French Minister, to induce King William to prevent Leopold's acceptance. Acting under the secret suggestion of the King, the father of Leopold, in a letter to the Spanish ambassador, withdrew the name of his son, as the election, under the circumstances, would not have the sincerity and spontaneity on which Leopold counted when he accepted the candidature. This note passing between Spain and the prince had not one word of France or of Prussia; and, as Gramont, the French Minister for Foreign Affairs, says in his "La France et la Prusse," far from settling affairs, complicated them, on the contrary, in the gravest manner. Explanations and guarantees for the future were demanded and refused, and thus began the Franco-Prussian war.*

As a result of this terrible collision, itself "the resultant of two nearly equal forces emanating from the Tuileries and the Vatican," the Napoleonic dynasty collapsed, the Papal temporal jurisdiction, no longer supported by French bayonets, disappeared, Italy was unified and regenerated, the German States were consolidated into an empire, and King William of Prussia was proclaimed Emperor of Germany within the Hall of Mirrors, in the palace of the French kings at Versailles, in the presence of the German princes, under the standards of the army before Paris (January 18, 1871).†

---

* A slab of stone at Ems contains this inscription: "13 Juli, 1870, 9 uhr, 10 minuten, Morgens." It was placed there to designate the precise spot and moment where and when Benedetti encountered the King and demanded the guaranties, and where the new German empire was born.

† Without passing positive judgment on the immediate responsibility for the war, usually ascribed to Empress Eugénie and her priestly advisers, which Jules Favre said was wickedly precipitated by the French Government, and which Gramont charges on Bismarck, one may be pardoned the remark that the conflict, the Iliad of unnumbered and unfinished woes, could have been very easily prevented by arbitration, or a little prudence, or the slightest concern for the welfare of the

peoples of the belligerent countries. In this struggle of dynastic ambitions and official selfishness the causes assigned are insignificant pretexts, wholly inadequate to justify the most momentous war of modern times. The testimony is conclusive that the Emperor Napoleon entered most reluctantly into the bloody arbitrament. M. le Baron de Susbielle, a general in the French army, a member of the military family of the Emperor, says that in the conferences just preceding hostilities Napoleon uniformly expressed his opposition and was sceptical as to the final issue. It is thought that Susbielle's memoirs, to be published after his death, will make interesting disclosures. Mr. Washburne, in his "Recollections of a Minister to France," bears concurrent testimony. "The truth is, that after eighteen years of peace the courtiers and adventurers who surrounded the Emperor seemed to think it was about time to have a war to awaken the martial spirit of the people. . . . If the Emperor had been left to himself the war would have been averted. I am quite sure his heart was never in the venture." Gramont's cautious statements are in the same direction. Phillimore (vol. i., p. 583) holds this language: "It may safely be affirmed that in the war of 1870 France was the aggressor, that the immediate reason which she assigned for beginning it was neither true nor adequate. The choice by the Spaniards of a Hohenzollern, by whomsoever suggested, for the throne of Spain, was not an act which disturbed the balance of power; it neither threatened the general liberties of Europe nor endangered the safety of France." On March 1, 1871, the Sovereign Assembly at Bordeaux, the organ of the national conscience and will, solemnly rendered the famous decree which proclaimed Napoleon III. and his dynasty "responsables de la ruine, de l'invasion et du demembrement de la France."

was that France was the stronger military power, and Leopold's declension was a welcome relief. His candidacy being removed, the strife for the throne became fiercer. On November 3, 1870, General Prim announced to the Cortes the Duke of Aosta, son of Victor Emmanuel, as the Ministerial candidate for the crown. Castelar impetuously denounced the attempt to put a foreigner over Spaniards. On the 15th, Amadeo was elected king, receiving on a vote by ballot a majority of seventy-one of those present and a majority of eighteen in a full house. The majority represented the Monarchists, who had combined to accomplish the revolution of September, 1868, and it was General Prim's vigor and popularity which brought about the election as an expedient for conciliating the monarchical sentiments of the more influential Spaniards. The desired effect was not produced. The choice excited no enthusiasm, elicited no applause, nor was a *viva* given by the multitude outside the building where the Cortes had made a sovereign. Thirty thousand troops, discreetly posted in principal thoroughfares, prevented any hostile demonstration, and the leading

Republicans, Figueras, Castelar, and Pi y Margall, advised against any acts of violence. Many journals condemned the Cortes. Grandees protested, placards caricatured and ridiculed. At theatres the dissent was openly expressed and strong. Spanish pride and hostility to foreigners were thoroughly aroused. Nevertheless, Zorrilla went to Italy to make the formal tender of the crown, and on January 2, 1871, the prince reached Madrid, and took the prescribed oaths of office in the presence of the regent, the Cortes, and the diplomatic corps. The ceremony was brief and simple. The reception by the populace was respectful and cold. The Provisional Government resigned, and a new ministry was appointed, embracing such men as Serrano, Martos, Moret, Sagasta, and Zorrilla. The Cabinet was a composite structure, a truce among rival factions, and represented the three principal monarchical parties which had been engaged in the revolution and which had united in the election of a new king. In Spain pensioners and dependents can easily be rallied in support of the Government, but in spite of that "coin d'avantage," the ministries were ephemeral

—eight in two years, one lasting seventeen days—failing in internal harmony and in the necessary strength to administer the government. Amadeo never had the friendship of the Carlists nor of the simon-pure Monarchists. The dynasty was offensive to the adherents of Don Carlos and of Alfonso, and to the Republicans, who were opposed to any king. After the death of Isabella, in 1503, the Castilian nobles were averse to the regency of Ferdinand, an alien to them, and they incited intrigue and conspiracy. So now, on the part of the old aristocracy there was an ill-concealed repugnance to an Italian king and to the queen. The Republicans, foreseeing the failure of the monarchy, were often consulting, so as to be forearmed and ready for the anticipated emergency. Even Zorrilla, then the President of the Council of Ministers and loyal to the King, on December 20, 1872, speaking of the reforms intended to prevent the outside world from confounding Spain with Turkey, said "they had something more to do than to patch up royal marriages or study Spanish interests from a dynastic point of view. Foreign powers could no longer say to our ambassadors that they merely represented the Queen's personal wishes."

Becoming convinced that the Opposition was irreconcilable, that factions were inevitable, that a stable ministry was impossible, Amadeo resolved on the singular course of abdicating the royal authority, and returning to the nation the powers with which he had been intrusted. Ferdinand resigned his regency to his son-in-law Philip with reluctance, under the pressure of immediate and successful revolt, but the act of this king was voluntary and against the ineffectual dissuasives of his Ministers. In a letter to the Cortes, February 11, 1873, he said: "I realize that my good intentions have been in vain. For two long years have I worn the crown of Spain, and Spain still lives in continual strife, departing day by day more widely from that era of peace and prosperity for which I have so ardently yearned. . . . I am to-day firmly convinced of the barrenness of my efforts and the impossibility of attaining my aims. These, deputies, are the reasons that move me to give back to the nation, and in its name to you, the crown offered to me by the national suffrage, renouncing it for myself, my children, and my successors." The nation and most of the leading statesmen were taken by surprise. A resignation of a throne seemed incredible. Changes in the ministry were habitual, but such a change, great and dynastic, was not looked for except through a revolution by soldiers. What to do in this sudden and critical emergency transcended the experience of the oldest, puzzled the sagacity of the wisest. The two branches of the Cortes assembled in one body, senators and deputies seated promiscuously, the President of the Senate occupying a place to the right of the President of the Congress, but the latter acting as the presiding officer of the Congress of Spain. Amid the uncertainty and confusion Castelar said, "The great problem is to ally order with liberty." The resignation was accepted unanimously, and in an address to his Majesty it was declared that he had been a most faithful observer of the respect due to the Chambers, and that he had kept most faithfully the oath taken when he accepted from the hands of the people the crown of Spain. It was further affirmed that the utmost efforts would have been made to induce the King to desist from his purpose, but they would have been vain before "the irresistible course of events." The Cortes therefore assumed "the supreme power and sovereignty of the nation," in order "to minister to the salvation of democracy, the base of the political structure of liberty, the soul of all our rights and of the country." It was said to the King, with a mixture of Spanish grandiloquence and chivalry, "While your Majesty remains upon our noble soil the Spanish people will offer you every mark of respect, of loyalty, and of deference, because it is due alike to your Majesty, to your virtuous and noble consort, and to your innocent children. The Spanish people cannot offer you a crown in the future, but when they have emerged from the difficulties that attend every epoch of transition and of crisis, they will then offer you another dignity, the dignity of a citizen in the midst of a free and independent people."*

---

* See Appendix A for an account of Fernando, Leopold, Amadeo, and the Duke of Montpensier.

CHAPTER V.

Difficulties of the Situation.—Establishment of the Republic.—Recognition by the United States.

THE abdication left the nation without executive head or authority. This was a *casus omissus,* an exigency unforeseen by the Constitution-makers. No provision had been made for such an interregnum. The ministry was *functus officio,* and disappeared with the authority of the king from whom the trust was derived. The Cortes therefore remained as the only legitimate and convenable source of political power. In the absence of Ferdinand VII. it had undertaken the national defence in "the epic years" from 1808 to 1814; it had abrogated the rights of Don Carlos; it had hastened the majority of Dona Isabel II.; it had recognized and sanctioned the dethronement of the Bourbon dynasty. It was now the most enduring power of Spanish nationality, and in this crisis came to the rescue of the country from anarchy and chaos. The Monarchists seemed to be wholly unprepared for the perplexing condition of affairs. The Republicans, on the other hand, had somewhat anticipated and prepared for it. Martos had said publicly on the 10th, "If the king goes, there is nothing else possible but the Republic." General Sickles, the American Minister, who was in full sympathy and constant consultation with the leaders, says the plans were well arranged, and the contingencies were provided for. As early as January 30th he had telegraphed to the Department at Washington for instructions in case the Cortes declared itself a convention, and appointed a new executive. Amid the distracted counsels, the terror, and the fearful apprehensions, the Republicans had patiently resisted all inducements to precipitate action, and had proceeded with much calmness and deliberation. In November, 1872, a law for the conscription of forty thousand men had provoked unusual opposition in the Cortes, and its execution met violent resistance in the provinces. Republican journals advised the use of the occasion for a serious attempt to overturn the monarchy, but a general convention of Republicans in Madrid, including Figueras, Castelar, and Pi y Margall, opposed any revolutionary movement. Some of these were Republicans from study and conviction, and were men of some civic experience and of large intellectual breadth. It was by them argued that a constitutional monarchy in the person of a queen by divine right had been found incompatible with personal liberty and national progress, and that the fruits of an elective monarchy were before them in the want of an executive. What was needed was an organization to hold human society together on principles of justice and right. Placing political power in the hands of a select family was irreconcilable with the great principle of national sovereignty in the people. To merge the sovereignty of a nation in a dynasty was an impossibility. It was necessary, therefore, that the Cortes, the sole existing available depositary of power, should at once proclaim the Republic, and leave to a Constitutional Convention, to be afterwards chosen, the duty of giving definitive form and organization. The first imperative duty was to organize such institutions as were needful to maintain social order. The two chambers resolved themselves into a National Assembly in permanent session and in the exercise of sovereign powers. By a vote of 258 to 32 this proposition was adopted. "The National Assembly, assuming all powers, declares the form of the government of the nation to be republican, leaving the organization of the form to a future convention." It has been objected that the establishment of the Republic had no constitutionality of origin or organization, but surely it had as much as the monarchy or any other regulation of family or class control. The old superstition of divine right of kings, that royalty never loses its right to reign, that no prescription or statute of limitations runs against royalty, can hardly claim respect or sanction since the English Revolution of 1688, the American Declaration of Independence or the French Revolution of 1789–1793. Besides, a republic appeared to be the only alternative, the way having been prepared by the proclamation of the natural rights of man, the denial of Bourbon or dynastic claims to supremacy, the enlargement of suffrage, the increasing freedom of worship, and the restriction of the powers of the Church. The executive power was constituted by ballot under the presidency of Estanislao Figueras, whose life had been consecrated to a republic. Castelar was chosen Secretary of State, Salmeron, Minister of Grace and Justice, and Pi y Margall, Minister of the Interior. After an election of a committee of the body to exercise the executive power, and of a larger committee to sit during the recess, the Cortes adjourned to await the meeting of the new Constituent Assembly.

The fall of the monarchy had not been the outcome of violence. Castelar said it was "without provocation from any one, without the fault of any one, the people or the Government, the Cortes or any public authority, without a cloud in the sky." "No one destroyed it. It died of natural causes. The monarchy died by internal decomposition. It dies by the providence of God. The Republic is the creation of circumstances. It comes from a conjuncture of society and nature and history." The Republic was accomplished legitimately. "It was not proclaimed in the streets; it was not the doing of a mob; it was not ushered in with disorder and tumult and blood: it was the work of a deliberative assembly, legitimate representatives of the people, substituting an executive authority for that which had ceased to exist by abdication of the King."

Having no moral support from European nations, which looked with disfavor on all extension of popular rights, Spain very naturally cast her eyes to the other side of the Atlantic, to the most advanced and enlightened of the countries which sprang from her bold enterprise, for sympathy and cheer in this supreme struggle. On the 12th, General Sickles had instructions from Washington to recognize the republican government when it was fully established and in possession of the power of the nation. He was to urge the expediency of emancipation in the West Indies, and of political reforms by efficient self-acting measures. Sickles subsequently urged the abolition of slavery in Cuba and self-government, but those in power could not grasp such schemes, or doubted their ability to carry them through. On the 13th, Cristino Martos, who had declined the Presidency of the Council of Ministers, was made President of the Sovereign Assembly, and General Sickles informed the Minister of State of his authority to recognize the Republic, and asked a public audience in his official character. On the 15th, the American Minister, in the uniform of a general of the Union Army, with two battalions of troops in line rendering military honors, the bands of music playing American national airs, had an imposing pageant as he went, thus escorted, to the reception chamber where awaited him the President and the Cabinet, to whom he read an address of congratulation and sympathy at " the establishment of a republic in the empire of Ferdinand and Isabella." " It is," he said, " a source of profound satisfaction that Spain finds in our example the means by which her prosperity and power may rest on sure foundations." President Figueras replied that he was deeply affected " by the mighty voice of the American people hailing with their benediction the advent of a republic, and he rejoiced in the strong bond of union between Spain, which carried to your shores the germs of civilization, and America which now gives us by her example the fruits of liberty and democracy." In behalf of those whose lives had been "devoted to the hard problem of uniting democracy and liberty," he expressed profound gratitude that there had been men who sought in the New World "a temple for their unfettered conscience, and founded a new order of society which has united in perfect equilibrium the authority of society with the inherent rights of man, the restless vigor of democracy with firm stability of power, the free outgrowth of all the aspirations of the human soul with respect for the laws and interests of others."* This official audience was followed by a visit to the palace of the Cortes, where, preceded by the mace-bearers and the secretaries, General Sickles was led to the *salon* of the President and presented to the Sovereign Assembly of Spain the fraternal salutations of the United States. On the whole, this was a fit and significant recognition; America hold-

---

* A far more conservative and orthodox declaration than the sentiment of Hubert Bancroft in "Popular Tribunals," which assumes the right of the governed, at all times, to instant and arbitrary control of the Government—"a dissolute principle of political ethics," which sanctions Dorrism, anarchy, lynch-law, and all democratic misrule.

ing up the hands of the infant republic in the country that sent out the discoverer—the daughter crowning the mother—the Government which made the contribution of soul-liberty, of divorced Church and State, to the science of politics, coming first and alone to give sympathy, encouragement, and moral support to the country of the Inquisition. Galileo may be put to death, but the world moves; the scaffold may have its political victims, but the cause of freedom advances. Sickles telegraphs, "Order assured; funds rising; confidence established." On March 6th the Congress, by joint resolution, in the name and on behalf of the American people, tenders its congratulations to the people of Spain upon their recent efforts to consolidate the principles of universal liberty in a republican form of government. This was in conformity to the established practice of the United States, to recognize foreign governments by reason of the fact of their existence as such, independent of any considerations of legitimacy or other political theory. The policy is not to interfere in any of the internal concerns of foreign powers, and to consider the Government *de facto* as the legitimate government. Claiming for ourselves the absolute right of self-constitution according to the national will, we cannot deny the same right to others, whether it be in harmony or in discord with our preferences. The moral and political support of the United States was helpful and opportune because the proclamation of the Republic was the signal and the occasion of the withdrawal of all the European powers except Switzerland from official relations with the new government. The executive was compelled to submit to the humiliation of treating with unaccredited agents of governments which refused to grant the mere naked status of a government. Monarchical sympathies and hostility to popular institutions doubtless influenced this suspension of diplomatic intercourse on the part of European nations, just as republican sympathies unquestionably induced the United States and Switzerland to act promptly in the opposite direction. At the Court of Madrid, Austria refuses all social and diplomatic intercourse with Mexico to-day, although a quarter of a century has elapsed since the execution of Maximilian, the alien invader. Governor Fish had cautiously instructed General Sickles: "It will be grateful to know that you have regarded the condition and prospects of the Republic such as to justify the discretionary power given you in that regard."

CHAPTER VI.

Presidents and Policy.—Overthrow of the Republic.—Rapid Changes.

The Monarchy having ceased from its own want of vitality, the Republic arose of its own virtue, by the law of necessity, a self-evolved product from existing causes. To return to the self-dethroned Amadeo was obviously impossible; to make a temporary regency was inexpedient; to try again the Bourbons would have been suicidal. From the inception of this republican movement it was uniformly declared that the assembly which proclaimed a republic must leave to a convention the duty of defining the organization. Opinions as to ultimate form and details were prudently kept in reserve until the assembling of a sovereign body convened for that specific purpose. However competent and indispensable the action of the Cortes had been, it was a temporary arrangement subject to approval, to revision if need be, to the rejection of the more authoritative constitutional assembly. The Government was but the delegation of the will of the Cortes. Elections were held in May for the Cortes Constituyéntes, and they resulted in the triumph of the Republican party. Nearly two hundred thousand electors exercised the right of suffrage in order and tranquillity, except where the Carlist insurgents disturbed the peace. The people sustained and confirmed the legitimacy of the Government in spite of the stereotyped cries so often heard in France and England —Unity is destroyed! Property is insecure! The Church is in danger!

The Council of Ministers elected by the Cortes had an executive head, called President of the Executive Power, and he has come to be called the President of the Republic. Estanislao Figueras, a trusted statesman, was the first, but after four months of unmanageable public disturbance he abandoned the office and withdrew in voluntary exile into France. Francisco Pi y Margall succeeded him and remained about six weeks. Nicholas Salmeron had an equally brief tenure, when Emilio Castelar came into office and was invested with powers that can hardly be said to have been nominated in the bond. The Republic had immense difficulties to overcome, and yet there was shown during its brief life some aptitude for government. Suffrage was established in a wider latitude and with less interference and dictation, natural rights were embodied in laws, popular sovereignty was enthroned as the true source of government, and religious liberty, without which there can be no true civil freedom, was "acclaimed in all its purity." The Minister of Grace and Justice, with the approval of the executive power, proposed to the Cortes, August 2, 1873, a bill for the absolute separation of Church and State. The National Assembly gave a unanimous vote for the immediate emancipation of slaves in Porto Rico, and the Republicans favored abolition in Cuba. Decrees were issued for the abolition of titles of nobility and the hereditary office of Grand Chancellor of the Indies. This had been created by Philip IV., and had been enjoyed almost continuously by the same family for two and a half centuries. The last incumbent was the Duke of Alba, brother of the Empress Eugénie. The duty of the chancellor was to collect a fee for authenticating every document, order, etc., relating to Spanish possessions in America. All previous attempts to get rid of the nuisance had failed. The advent of the Republic was required to accomplish the needed reform. The general purpose of the Republic was to secure to the people a real electoral liberty, to prevent undue official and bureaucratic influence, to punish with equal severity the violent pressure of political parties and of the mob, to combine order, law, and liberty, to put an end to African slavery in the Colonies, and follow emancipation by cognate reforms as the best means of restoring peace and prosperity to the islands.

Congress having rejected a proposition approving the conduct of the Government during the parliamentary recess, President Castelar, at 5.30 A.M. on January 3, 1874, resigned his office. While the Cortes were engaged in the election of his successor, they were dispersed by troops of the garrison under the command of General Pavia, who took possession of the palace and occupied the other public buildings and the principal thoroughfares. In the memorandum, January 25, 1874, signed by Sagasta, which the "Executive Power of the Spanish Republic" addressed to the foreign powers, it is said, "The garrison of Madrid with wonderful prevision seized the moment for interference, rightly interpreting the wishes of the army, the navy, and the whole country, thereby saving in a few hours the life and honor of the nation." This *coup-d'état* was followed by a provisional government, a dictatorship, under Francisco Serrano, who used the same designation of "President of the Executive Power of the Republic." Martial law was proclaimed, and the expulsion by superior military authority was justified on the pretext of a "grave peril which menaced social order and liberty after the vote of censure passed by the Chamber against the policy of the Ministry presided over by Señor Castelar." In two months Marshal Serrano was invested with, or assumed practically, absolute power as Chief of State. A decree of the Council separated the functions of the President of the Executive Power from those of the President of the Council, conferred an unlimited presidency upon Serrano, and clothed him with extraordinary powers.

It would be difficult if not impossible to justify such an arbitrary seizure by any principles having the sanction of publicists or civilized public opinion, yet in Spain parties and politics cannot be measured by the rules which obtain elsewhere. If we refuse to judge Isabella the Catholic, and her confessor, Torquemada, and the papal upholding of the Inquisition by the Christianity of the present day, so we are constrained to apply modified or elastic standards to governmental procedure in Spain. One of the chiefest peculiarities in Spain, and at the same time one of the main hinderances to a republic or to a good government, is the wellnigh universal recognition of the legitimacy of a resort to military power in order to change the administration or accomplish political reforms. Such Republicans as Castelar repudiate pronunciamentos and the like arbitrary agencies, but generally Conservatives and Liberals, Carlists and Republicans, accept, apply, or submit to such expedients for attaining their ends, and no party in Spain can find fault with others in that respect. General Cushing, in 1875, wrote, "All parties, one after the other, have had recourse to conspiracy, violence, and usurpation in order to attain their personal or party ends. It was by military violence that Prim, Serrano, and Topete overthrew Queen Isabel. It was by military violence that Serrano became President by the will of Pavia... So that neither the militarism nor the illegality of the movement tends in the least degree to repel the acceptance of it in any part of the country. And quite as little repulsion is produced by the suddenness of the movement or the brief time occupied in its consummation. On the night of February 11, 1873, all Spain went to bed a Monarchy and woke up a Republic. In like manner, on January 2, 1874, the Republican dictatorship of Castelar disappeared in a night to give place to the Conservative dictatorship of Serrano. On the morning of December 31, 1874, it did not appear at all extraordinary to the Spaniards in waking up to find that the Republic had vanished and the Monarchy returned with the dramatic celerity of a change of scenery at the opera." Those who overthrew the Republic used the army to "satisfy the instinct of self preservation," "patriotically saved a dictatorship," and claimed that they were identified with the revolution of 1868, "with the political significance of that glorious uprising," and that they were united on the basis of a democratic code in the Constitution of 1869, "in the enjoyment of the liberties which it concedes, and above all in the strict and vigilant use of the guarantees with which it surrounds the cause of order." Outside of Spain such language seems to be the distempered ravings of intoxication, and is antipodal to the action it vindicates; but in Spain politics and public opinion have a rule and standard of their own. Constitutional limitations have no force. Supposed political necessity justifies any assumption. Discretion is the measure of power, and Mr. Calhoun's aphorism finds confirmation that there is no difference between a government having all power and a government having the right to take what powers it pleases.

5

CHAPTER VII.

Causes of the Fall.—Account of the Presidents.—Abrupt Transition.—The Army.—False Hopes.—Madrid.

To one desiring the permanence of the republic and thinking that form of government the most successful in attaining justice and freedom, it is natural to inquire anxiously into the causes which led to such a sudden disappointment of hopes, such a rapid collapse of a government having promise of stability in its inherent rightness and in the ability of its leaders. When Prim was asked why he did not establish a republic in 1868, he replied, "It would have been a republic without republicans." In 1873 there seemed to exist a strong republican feeling, but the governmental policy of Spain has never been favorable to the growth of republican practices, to the training of the people for democratic institutions, to familiarizing them with home rule, individual judgment, personal independence. A republic is the highest development of civil government. In a monarchy a few capable men may rule; in a republic the many are to govern, and need to be continually disciplined for their high functions. To this general cause of want of training may be superadded errors of leaders, divisions in ranks, and still other reasons beyond the control of those charged with the administration. For centuries Spain had had a monarchy, class interests with titles and privileges, and an ecclesiastical hierarchy in full accord with monarchy and aristocracy, and often in shameful tolerance of their vicious practices. The traditions of the country, the social influence, the literature, the schools, the Church presiding over infancy, marriage and death, the wealth, were all adverse to popular government. The principles of politics represented in a republic are distasteful to royalty and to dominant classes. Besides the Monarchists there were the Carlists, bitter, reactionary, irreconcilable, with journals, villages, and a willing priesthood at their back. The military organization, compact, mobile, subordinate to ambitious, conspiring officers, was the enemy of the Republic. In the Peninsula revolutions have been chronic, and property always dreads disorder, sudden changes, anarchy. The feudal system had been but partially extirpated. Civil and ecclesiastical jurisdiction was only partially limited and defined. The revenue system, with custom-houses at frontiers and *octroi* tolls in every town, was then as now corrupt, and the boldest and best shrank from an attempt to reform the abuses. National expenditures exceeded income, and pensions and civil list and contracts made a horde of greedy dependants. Bureaucracy flourished in worst form. The situation was environed with almost superhuman difficulties, and obvious reforms for admitted and deplored abuses seemed impossible. The hostile interests and opinions became active. In Great Britain and the United States we see what arguments and combinations can do to sustain monopolies, trusts, and legalized wrongs. In France, in the journals and utterances of public men we have an illustration anew of the old fable of the lamb in the stream below muddying the water for his lupine majesty above. Everything done by the Republic is perverted. Everything favorable to regulated liberty is decried. Everything that tends to popular government is discredited and opposed. Every little popular disturbance or lawlessness is distorted and magnified and made to exceed in enormity centuries of tyranny and cruelty and horrible wrong by royalty, aristocracy, and the Church, with their selfish and venal minions, and all possible factions and divisions are fomented. Every disorder, defeat, international complication, is hailed with joy. The Monarchists are enemies in the camp. Patriotism is secondary to self-aggrandizement and to the restoration of a dynasty. Nothing is left undone to discredit the Republic and to make it a failure, to produce crises, to promote obstruction and confusion, and to create an apparent necessity for the coming back of the *ancien régime*, and so in Spain. The enemies of the new government availed themselves of the army and of every agency for its overthrow. It ought to be added that during the Republic three wars were in progress—the Cuban war, the Federalist in the South, and the Carlist. The last was so important and formidable as to demand for its suppression the coalition of all parties, and the concentration of every energy. And hence, until that object was attained, the Republicans felt constrained to postpone reforms in the military service, reduction in public expenditures, diminution of useless offices, reduction of the enormous pension list, separation of Church and State, abolition of slavery, and the adaptation of the Constitution to a republican form of government.

The fall of the Republic is so often used as an argument conclusive against the adaptedness of such a form of government to European peoples that a fuller consideration of the causes may not be inappropriate.

(a) The first suggestion, obviously, is as to the Presidents on whom the people relied and to whom naturally all eyes were turned. Each alternately was looked to as the Palinurus to guide the ship of State between Scylla and Charybdis and amid the storms. They were not men of executive capacity or constructive faculties. They had been political seers, eloquent theorists, advanced thinkers in the science of human rights and remedies, but they were deficient in the genius of common-sense, in the mastery of details, in the rare endowment of adapting government and laws to novel and sudden emergencies.

Estanislao Figueras was the first. An adroit parliamentarian, a loyal Republican, a man of integrity, a disciple of Proudhon, he lacked firmness of purpose and strength of will. Hesitating, irresolute, letting " I dare not" wait upon " I would," he became discouraged, his heavy responsibilities confused and intimidated him, and he abandoned his post. For two days he was sought in vain, and afterwards "turned up" a refugee in France. He had a habit, when President, of rising at five o'clock in the morning, and of going at that early hour to his office. The Madrilenos, indignant at this overthrow of their practices, declared that if he thought to oblige them to rise so early, he deceived himself, for it would only turn out that they would retire a little later. And, in fact, a number of politicians went to salute the President before they sought their beds.

Francisco Pi y Margall is a man of first-rate ability, a writer of classical purity, an historian of art, a profound lawyer, and is now engaged, as is Castelar, in writing a history of Spain. He is German in his type of thinking, and is deficient in the arts of the successful politician. Proudhon is also his ideal, and he follows to the extreme his economic or socialistic theories. Apparently he accepts his master's brochure, *le principe fédératif*, and would organize the nation, if not wider peoples, by a reciprocal agreement among individuals and communities. He is a protectionist, and would be a tyrant, as were those of ancient Greece, if he were not restrained by his benevolence of heart, which makes him incomparable as a man but unsafe as a governor. At a meeting of the Republicans of Madrid, in February, 1888, to celebrate the anniversary of the Republic, he gave a programme of his views, in which he said he desired freedom of work, emancipation of municipalities, compulsory and gratuitous education, abolition of lotteries, "suppression of the budget of worship," and the appropriation of the eight million dollars paid to the clergy to the establishment of elementary, normal, and industrial schools. Obstinate in his personal convictions, in the conclusions of the closet, by a singular incongruity of character he has much credulity and flexibility in the presence of men. His accession to the presidency awakened strong expectations that he would develop into a broad-minded, successful statesman, and that what Figueras from inertness failed to do Pi would achieve in excess. Fatal illusion! His ephemeral exaltation contracted an horizon previously too narrow. At the utmost, a good administrator in peaceful times; a Cavour, a Bismarck, never. General Sickles, at the beginning of the Republic, said of him that he was in personal appearance and in many traits of character, intellectual and moral, like Mr. Calhoun, and was universally regarded as a trustworthy officer and a good citizen. Some months later he said that Pi y Margall abandoned power because he was unwilling to stop disintegration by force, and unable to prevent it by timely political action.

Nicolas Salmeron, now a professor in the university at Madrid, is a doctrinaire, a savant, a philosopher, an ideologist. It seemed to him easy to transfer into practical life the captivating speculations of his great German masters, and he presented them, first as deputy then as minister, with a manly eloquence. He knows little of financial or economic questions, and prefers his books and lecture-room to the hard realities of political conflicts. In 1887 he resigned as deputy because of not being in accord with his electors in their radicalism.

EMILIO CASTELAR.—It is not easy to write impartially of this eminent and excellent man. In Spain, in America, in the civilized world, he is renowned as a rhetorician and an orator. Even his political enemies (he has no personal ones) concede immense excellence as an orator. His friends rank him among the most distinguished speakers of all time. On December 20, 1872, after a speech from Castelar in favor of abolishing slavery in Porto Rico, the Minister of State (Martos), himself no mean orator, closed the debate thus, " The debate is closed. Señor Castelar has spoken the last word—the slaves in Porto Rico are already free. The bill the Government will bring in can only give legal sanction and form to the inspired utterance of the world's greatest orator." On February 7, 1888, after a speech in the Congress, business was perforce suspended, the boisterous hurrahs were continued for fifteen minutes, congratulations greeted from all sides of the chamber, and Sagasta, the Prime-minister—the same Sagasta who as Minister of State, in an official paper in 1874, had spoken contemptuously of "his arrogant self-conceit and ill-restrained demagogism"—left the Government bench, crossed the hall, embraced the speaker, and warmly commended his patriotism and eloquence. The eloquence lacks spontaneity; it is studied and dramatic, and labors for immediate applause. The day, the hour, the audience, everything is prearranged. You laugh, you cry, you surrender yourself to the enchantment, but the speeches are seldom embodied into political acts, into laws. The god of speech is not a statesman. Castelar is an egoist and very vain. The common caricature in the shop-windows is a peacock with spread tail and Castelar's head. The popular nickname is *embolado*, a bull with balls on his horns. A rival said of him that he so coveted the *digito monstrari* that he never saw a marriage without wishing to be the bride, nor a funeral without wishing to be the corpse.

His short trial as President was a series of misadventures and failures. He planned, but the plans came to grief. He failed to remodel the army, was clumsy in the *Virginius* controversy, quailed before the Pope in the appointment of some bishops, was not courageous in executing his emancipation views, and had inextricable disorder in administration. Nothing was done with his bill separating Church and State, and his draft of a federal constitution showed little acquaintance with politics and government. In fact, the Spanish Republic had no Morris, no Hamilton, no Madison, no Washington.

As a Republican, Castelar has lost much of his following, and an invisible thread is the only tie that binds him to his party. His old associates say that but for the remembrances of the ancient tribune of the people he would be a liberal Monarchist. This judgment is harsh and unjust. For years he has been in Europe the ablest and most conspicuous advocate of popular rights, of freedom of religion, and recently, with emphasis, affirmed that he was a Republican, heart and mind and soul, but favored the coming of a republic by evolution instead of by revolution.* By what process a republic can be

---

* The ill-advised mutiny of 1886 was a clear gain for Mon-

evolved without a compact, aggressive Republican party in the active use of the usual agencies for exposing errors and wrongs and enlightening public opinion, history gives us no light. Certainly it will never be evolved by chance, nor as the outcome of, nor by acquiescence in, the domination of royalty, class interests and prerogatives, and the alliance of civil and ecclesiastical power. Castelar may not keep pace with some wild modern iconoclasts and Nihilists and Anarchists, but whoever has watched with hope and sympathy the great unceasing, varying struggle for freedom in Europe, battle-scarred, debt-oppressed, Church-crushed, conscience-enslaved,

---

archy and a serious blow to Republicanism. Castelar published a letter respecting the revolt, and the tone of it shows a feeling of bitterness as well as of regret. He says,

"I denounce with all the energy of my soul the last military sedition, it being my firmest conviction that *pronunciamientos*, even if they should triumph under the name and advocacy of our Republic, will lead us to the Cæsarian Prætorianism of old Rome, not to liberty and democracy. I have said, and I repeat it now, that events like those most deplorable ones of Monday last justify our being denominated the Turkey of the West. I reaffirm my resolution to accept the tremendous responsibility of power only when the people legally convoked, or the Cortes legally constituted, demand this by an express vote."

royalty-ridden, class-dominated Europe, can have only generous charity and exalted admiration for one whose pure life and cultivated intelligence and large ability and quenchless zeal and burning eloquence have been consecrated as the John the Baptist of the gospel of universal emancipation.

A republic, the rational logic of enlightened public authority, with agents having the indecision of Figueras, the pliancy of Pi y Margall, the ideologism of Salmeron, the theatrical spirit of Castelar, had not a hopeful outlook. Men are but the embodiments of thoughts, and nearly all great enterprises and institutions crystallize around individual men. In critical moments great actors have the *elan*, the prophecy, the prestige of success. In all countries, especially in those accustomed to monarchical institutions, the people find the reflection of their lives, their interests, their glories, in a dynastic entity or in a hero. Other more potent causes than the weakness, the nullity, of the chiefs contributed to the failure. In the absence of these the Republic would have survived presidential incompetency; these causes, vital and operative, the Republic would have perished even under the vigorous leadership of such a man as Prim.

(b) As a second cause may be mentioned the abrupt transition from a monarchy. The people had had no preliminary training in self-government, nor any sufficient democratic education. Amadeo leaving Spain without a government, the Republicans possessed themselves of it, but did not know what to do with it, and did not comprehend the exigencies and responsibilities of the new and sudden situation. What kind of a republic was it to be? What the form and functions of the organism? and what kind of a head of the executive power? were serious questions. Shall the President be chosen for a long term and be re-eligible, or for a short term? In our Washington the monarchical traditions, which sat very loosely, were easily broken, and the union of States was formed and consolidated under a written, previously adopted, organic law. In the South American republics, as remote from the monarchical centre as we were, but without our home-rule training and our inheritance of English law and liberties, there have been struggles, contentions, tentative experimentations (not yet ended) before reaching tranquillity and order. The measures adopted were trivial, or not pushed to proper results, or not put upon a high plane. The press was free, but instead of serious discussions there were license and incendiarism. Primary schools were neglected. Political associations were noisy and aimless, rather than practical or valuable. The wisdom that was hoped for did not come, and in these un-Minerva-like days had not time to come.

(c) The badly organized army remained in *statu quo*. This instrument of peace and order, when it is rightly controlled and disciplined, had not been taught its true position of subordination, and had not the sense of obedience. The time was, besides, unpropitious for military reforms. Three wars, as has been stated, were in progress against Cuban, Carlist, and federal insurgents. Soldiers and their officers were ignorant of the first principles of Republicanism, and of the true duties of men organized and armed at public expense. They regarded themselves as the sovereigns of the nation, the true arbiters of its destiny, as the saviors, and hence claimed the right to rule. *Inter arma silent leges.*

The supremacy of the civil over the military was a surprising and an offensive doctrine, and they complained and conspired. The monarchy was preferred as giving opportunities for promotion, and they coveted the decorations, the nobiliary titles, the gala festivities, the sudden advancements. Every man educated in the military schools was a Monarchist. All waited for an occasion to show hostility to the Republic, and it was not long in coming. General Pavia, who himself had participated in the insurrection of 1866, was selected as the willing agent for the overthrow. Any other bold, ambitious officer would have done as well. The blow was struck. It was fatal.

(*d*) Hope disappointed maketh the heart sick. After the excitement and the disappointment of Quixotic expectations, there ensued with the masses a lassitude of mind and weariness of spirit. The change in the government did not supersede the need of labor, nor take away poverty and suffering. People who were Republicans were disheartened, and sank into apathy. Capital and credit were frightened, and there were repeated announcements that taxes must be increased.

Carlism was defiant and confident; the federal movement was protracted; municipalities were in rebellion; disturbances were unchecked; finances were in disorder. The people were fatigued, willing for a change, and would have abandoned themselves to any adventurer or usurper. The inherited Mussulman fatalism reasserted itself, and the act of brutal force, of positive treason, encountered no resistance.

(*e*) Another cause hastening the downfall is the unique condition of Madrid, whose inhabitants live on the Government, and by whose favor they consume largely of the public revenues. Bureaucracy, centralization, official corruption, find theatre and stimulus in the capital. The contesting parties form among themselves a kind of society of mutual succor, and there is a great company of pensioners, dependants, and hungry expectants. As the head and heart of the nation, Madrid is the seat and focus of the conspiracy of the Conservatives and the Liberals to preserve the dominance of the capital and keep up the source of supply of spoils and *tripotage*. Reforms, here as elsewhere in Spain, in the civil administration are wellnigh impossible because the political parties and many prominent leaders are interested directly or indirectly in the continuance of the abuses. The Republic threatened the trade of the image-makers, and they were clamorous for its overthrow. The Passion play at Ober-Ammergau makes the money-changers, expelled with cords from the temple, the active, unscrupulous instigators of the resistance to the Saviour, and the prompters and bribers of Judas in the betrayal. To cleanse the Augean stable and check the infamy of life of priests and prelates, even the fearless spirit of Innocent was unable. It was easier to crush by fire and sword the heresy fed by the scandals.

CHAPTER VIII.

Pronunciamento for Alfonso.

MEANWHILE the dictatorship continued to administer public affairs in the name and under the external forms of a republic; but there were constant croppings-out of tendencies or purposes looking to the re-establishment of the monarchy in the person of Don Alfonso, son of Isabel, or of some foreign prince.

The change from Castelar to Serrano did not suspend diplomatic intercourse with the United States. In accordance with the rule of action in cases of change of authority, General Cushing presented his credentials. The European powers continued to abstain from recognition. Under the initiation of Germany, they came to perceive the wisdom of the policy observed by the Union, but were restrained by the perverse refusal of Russia to change her attitude.

Whatever may have been the intentions

of Serrano's Government, there was an impossibility of action in many matters of domestic or internal reform. The war against the Carlists had been going on with various fortunes when the tranquillity and apparent security at Madrid were disturbed by a pronunciamento from a detachment of the army, commanded by Martinez de Campos, in favor of the enthronement of Don Alfonso de Borbon. The great body of the Army of the North was in ready sympathy with this movement. The Government fell without a struggle for existence. On December 31, 1874, there was announced a regency ministry under the presidency of the lately imprisoned Antonio Canovas del Castillo, a statesman of comprehensive views, high character, and of great ability. The late Ministers and the Republicans remained undisturbed in Madrid. There was general acquiescence in the change. Public authorities sent in their adhesion. The army, the most potential of all the factors in Spanish politics, gave its cordial support. Alfonso was introduced by a pronunciamento similar to General Monk's action in England, and the intruding or usurping government, not chosen by the

Cortes, was accepted as legitimate. The Liberal Constitution of 1869 was ignored as a nullity, and that of 1845 was accepted because of the abdication of Isabel and her assent in various forms to the accession of Alfonso. Universal suffrage had been a distinguishing feature; Canovas suppressed and substituted qualifications which excluded half the voters. It needs to be repeated in connection with this usurpation and nullification of law that Spanish statesmen seem to have no conception of regular constitutional government, and expect changes, not so much by orderly, prescribed processes of succession or election or legislation as by the means of tumultuary uprisings or the demands of soldiers. In a published manifesto, Alfonso was made to profess ideas of constitutional administration, and yet among his first political acts was the acceptance of the new Syllabus of the Vatican. By royal decrees, certain real property held by the State was restored to the Church, and the clergy were again charged on the public treasury. This favoritism towards the religious orders was of a piece with the general reaction against the more liberal and advanced views of the recent governments.

"The right of public assembly was abrogated, free instruction was abolished, the Jesuit schools were re-established, and liberal professors were expelled" from the universities.

These royal ordinances, or pragmatica, so alien to our notions of government, have been claimed by most European sovereigns as the prerogative of the supreme legislators of their kingdoms. They are sometimes mere executive orders, sometimes supplementary to legislative enactments, but have been perverted into arbitrary acts of tyranny, and have become "effectual levers" for thwarting the popular or legislative will, or for "overturning the liberties of the nation."

CHAPTER IX.

Constitution of 1876.—Freedom of Worship in Spain.

The new Government, with deliberation, undertook in 1876 the preparation of a constitution, which was submitted and adopted, and is now the Constitution of the Government of Spain. Its prominent features are hereditary monarchy in the person and family of Don Alfonso XII., and a legislative assembly of two branches, the Senate and the Congress. The Senate, while not, as the House of Lords, a devolving of the right to a share of legislative power by mere hereditary succession, is an aristocratic body composed of three classes. 1. Senators in their own right, such as sons of the King, grandees of Spain having a fixed income of sixty thousand pesetas, captains-general of the army, admirals of the navy, the Patriarch of the Indies, archbishops, etc. 2. One hundred persons nominated by the Crown for life. 3. One hundred and fifty persons elected by the corporations and the larger taxpayers. Numbers 2 and 3 are to be taken from certain prescribed political, military, literary, titular, or proprietary classes. The Congress of Deputies, founded on general suffrage, regulated by the law of elections, consists of persons chosen for five years by electoral districts, in the proportion of one deputy to every fifty thousand of the population.

A step in advance was taken on the Church question. Article XI. reads thus: "The Catholic Apostolic Roman religion is that of the State. The nation obliges itself to maintain the worship and its ministers. No person shall be molested in the territory of Spain for his religious opinions, nor for the exercise of his particular worship, saving the respect due to Christian morality. Nevertheless, no other ceremonies nor manifestations in public will be permitted than those of the religion of the State."

This cautious provision of toleration was opposed vehemently in both branches of the Cortes, Señor Martinez Izquierdo (the bishop who was assassinated by a priest at the vestibule of a church in Madrid, April 18, 1886), taking the lead in the opposition; but it passed by a large majority, having had the cordial support of Canovas.

Bergson, the French translator of Heffter's "International Law," speaking "de les rapports de l'Église et de l'État" in France, says that the former exclusive protection in favor of the Catholic Church has undergone a profound modification, viz., that "to the political principle of the unity of faith has succeeded the social principle of the liberty of conscience and religion." A somewhat similar modification of the former exclusive favor of the Roman Catholic Church has occurred in Spain. The temporal power is pledged to the maintenance of the Catholic Apostolic Roman religion, but a protection is guaranteed to all Spanish subjects against ill usage from the Catholic Church or from any other interfering power. The full force of the last clause of the article has elicited discussion from statesmen and lawyers. It is ambiguous, evasive, susceptible of an oppressive interpretation, and in terms restricts the liberty of all dissenting worship to private houses. A recent instance of "sharp practice" and of violation of parental rights in Vigo, shows that there is need of a clearer definition and of a better guarantee.* The article is far from being *en rapport* with New Testament or American ideas of liberty of worship, but it has, under progressive statesmanship and the enlightenment of the nineteenth century, been so construed as to allow a greatly improved measure of religious freedom. At the funeral services of the Emperor William and the Emperor Frederick in the Lutheran chapel at Madrid, the diplomatic corps, the Ministry, military and civil

---

* The *Temps* of February, 1888, reproduced in the London *Times*, gives the case of a young lady, in possession of a small fortune, who entered a convent in defiance of the wishes of her father, who alleged that his daughter was a minor, and in very bad health. The severities of the novitiate and religious excitement increased her illness. Medical men advised her immediate withdrawal from the convent. The superior refused her consent, and the bishop declined to interfere. An order compulsory was obtained; but on the morning of the day of the removal the girl was induced to take perpetual vows. This put an end to civil interference, doors were shut against the father, and eight days after the girl died. All the property at her disposal, 70,000 francs, was bequeathed to the convent.

The Spanish Church Aid Society, in its last annual report, 1888, mentions the arrest and condemnation to two years and four months' imprisonment of one of their pastors, Señor Vila, for publishing a reply to an attack of a priest on the Protestants.

dignitaries, and Infante Don Antonio, were present in showy uniforms. Public opinion is often in advance of, and better and stronger than, law. "No system, however elaborate, and no contrivance, however ingenious, can be finally effective for the preservation of personal liberty, without the constant assistance of an enlightened, healthy, and vigorous public sentiment." An established Church, *ex vi termini,* implies unjust discrimination against other churches, governmental favoritism, inequality, usurpation, wrong. To establish one sect or denomination or Church puts the stamp of disfavor, of inferiority, on those not established. If no evils accrued, if no injustice were done, still the alliance of Church and State, the civil support of a religion, transgresses the legitimate province and function of the civil power. There is only one safe rule for the people, for the weak, for minorities, against civil or ecclesiastical tyranny. If there be no purpose to injure, let it be put beyond the power to do so. The history of States and Churches leaves no room for doubt as to what will come of the power to suppress dissent when passion or prejudice or interest dictates the use of force. When a religion or a church is once "established," or adopted by a State, intolerance and a long train of evils are inevitable. There is no instance to the contrary. History teaches but one lesson. Repugnance of persecution to the spirit of Christ, to the teachings of the New Testament, has never been a hinderance; and uniformity has been invariably sought by using without scruple the means seemingly most effective. Clearest intellects, kindliest tempers, and piety have favored cruelest tortures. When the belief that persecution for conscience' sake is sinful is denounced as heresy, to be visited with the full penalties of that unpardonable crime,* then there is no limit to ecclesiastical jugglery and wrong; as Henry George says, "Aggression grows by what it feeds on, and the idea of justice is blurred by the habitual toleration of injustice."

In its general provisions the Constitution corresponds in theory to the constitutions of other monarchical countries. It is a com-

---

* Lea's "History of the Inquisition of the Middle Ages," vol. i., p. 224.

promise seeking a *juste milieu* between reactionary, intolerant, ultramontane Monarchists, the absolutism of Bourbonism, on the one hand, and radical democracy, on the other. There is sufficient flexibility of language, under Spanish precedents, to "allow ample room for the healthful play of parties;" and during the twelve years of its existence Spain has had the Conservatism of Canovas, and the Liberalism of Sagasta and Moret, has survived several military revolts, almost annihilated Carlism, and passed securely over the crisis of a transition from a Bourbon king to the regency of an Austrian woman.

In the frequent changing constitutions there seems to be no comprehension of the fundamental distinction between the constitution-making and the law-making power. It is doubtful whether the ordinary Spanish statesman could understand the checks and balances and limitations which are discussed with such consummate ability by Calhoun in his "Disquisition on Government and the Constitution of the United States." In Spain, a royal decree, a legislative act, suspends or abrogates the Constitution, and there is no remedy except by an uncertain election or a military *émeute*. A court of last resort, with original or appellate jurisdiction, to afford adequate relief when limits of constitutional grant have been exceeded by Sovereign or Cabinet or Cortes, is a need yet to be supplied in Spanish jurisprudence.

CHAPTER X.

Cabinet Government.

The Constitution of 1812 made the initiative in the formation of a parliamentary government, by dividing the functions of the executive power into seven responsible Ministries. Each of these was made responsible to the Cortes for the decrees countersigned, and was not permitted to plead a command of the King in excuse for official action. Decisions not so countersigned were null. The highest court of justice was invested with jurisdiction in the trial of Ministers and of high functionaries. This Constitution was abrogated by kingly usurpation and foreign interference, but it is interesting as the genesis of an effort to naturalize in Spain the governmental ideas which have become so valuable in Great Britain. By successive trials the Government has become, in large degree, a government of the Ministry sustained by the Congress, thus in theory placing the legislative and executive power ultimately in the hands of a majority of the voters. The Sovereign is the fountain of honor, the source of pardons, but has no constitutional power in making or annulling laws. The Queen-regent presides once a week in the Council of Ministers, and takes an intelligent interest in the affairs of the kingdom, but acts within her limited sphere of a constitutional sovereign, and carefully abstains from dictation or an attempt to control. The President of the Council of Ministers, or Prime-minister, at present has no portfolio as in England, but is the recognized head of the Government and has a general supervision over all affairs of the nation. Being invited so to do by the Sovereign, he selects his colleagues in the Cabinet, who are officially proclaimed by royal order. Each Minister must be a member of the Cortes (he is not so *ex officio*), but is not required on appointment to have his official life renewed or confirmed by the indorsement of a constituency. In both Houses a Minister can sit, debate, introduce measures, but can vote only in the body of which he is a member. In Senate and in Congress a front bench to the right of the President is reserved for the Ministers of the Crown, and each Minister is expected to explain and defend the measures emanating from, or specially connected with, his department. Sometimes, in a general debate or a particular discussion, the Prime-minister sums up or concludes. The Constitution provides for "interpellation"—a method somewhat akin to the questions propounded in the House of Commons. Any member of the Cortes can question a Minister, demand an interpellation, or propose a vote of censure or want of confidence. Such a vote, however, does not, of necessity, result in a change of Government; it has no legal effect, and the Ministry, in the face of it, may continue in office. The Crown, under the Constitution, may appoint and dismiss Ministers and dissolve the Cortes. The two Houses are inhibited from deliberating together. The Government is required to present every year to the Cortes, for examination and discussion, the general budget of the expenditures of the State, accompanied by the plan of taxation and the proposed means of meeting the expenditures; but the laws on taxes and public credit must be presented first to the Congress of Deputies. As parliamentary procedure attracts so much attention, it may be mentioned as of curious interest that instead of committees at the beginning of every session of the Cortes, each body is divided by lot into sections, to which projects of laws are referred. After discussion and action, the sections report through commissions. These sections, except the one having charge of the Budget, are recast every month or two by a new allotment. In the regular debate the speakers are listed, *pro* and *con*, but are not limited as to time. There is no hour rule nor previous question. Each speaker can "rectify," and with Spanish loquaciousness this "system of oratorical ramifications" makes debate tedious and an issue remote.

CHAPTER XI.

Progress of Liberal Institutions in Spain.—Platform of Liberal and Conservative Parties.

THE American idea of the derivation of political power from the people has not found lodgment, as an actuality, in Spanish politics, literature, or thought. The Constitution contains no declaration of rights, no abstract enunciation of fundamental truths and principles. What was once, rather sneeringly, ridiculed as Virginia and Carolina "abstractions," theoretical annunciations of essential truths, inalienable rights, the bases of sound government and individual liberty, is what Spaniards need to comprehend and accept. Carefully defined distributions and limitations of power have not been thought necessary to prevent encroachments. There is imperative need of a sounder opinion on the proper means of changing the Ministry and the Constitution. All parties have resorted to conspiracies, and no party can cast the first stone in condemnation of others. Absolute monarchy, constitutional monarchy, elective monarchy, a republic, a regency, civil dictatorship, military dictatorship, have come and gone with suddenness and celerity. Militarism, usurpation, flagrant violations of constitutions and laws, oscillations between despotism and anarchy, have marked the unhappy history of this century, and the people have often quietly acquiesced in these rapidly occurring mutations as things to be expected in the course of human events. Power has been sought, not by legal methods or through constitutional forms, but by revolts, insurrections, conspiracies. The bayonet has superseded the ballot-box or a vote of the Cortes. The army has been a political engine. Military officers have been intriguers. Castelar once said that in the crisis of every party question the inquiry is, Which controls the *cannons?*

Still, the impartial student of the science of politics can see much to encourage. A comparison between 1808 and 1888 will show gratifying progress. Liberty is of slow growth. For centuries the political systems of Europe have been founded upon partial rights and privileges, but the advance is easily discovered. The manners, the ideas, the passions moulded during past ages, do not readily yield. Austria, the most feudal State, has been forced into lines of constitutional government, and has found it necessary to modify concordats and reconstruct the empire-kingdom in harmony with modern ideas. As far back as 1861, a citizen Ministry came into power, of which only three bore aristocratic names. The Tory party in England has become conservative, and is adopting many liberal views and measures. The full scope of the process of transformation cannot be measured ; but we see reform in suffrage and representation, an advance towards local government in the counties, and, contemporaneously, a hopeful discussion as to the need of a change in the constitution of the House of Lords. A remarkable fact, similar to the one mentioned in Austria, exists in Spain in 1888, where all the nine Ministers, the President of the Congress, and nearly all the sub-secretaries are from the people. Nearly every man of eminence in the dominant party, and very many in the Opposition, owe their elevation and influence, not to royal favor or aristocratic birth, but to splendid abilities and the "openings" which have come from the popular ideas incorporated into the government—embodied in a representative constitution.

Parties are exponents of tendencies and principles when they embody, not sectional hate nor dead issues, but living practical questions. In governments tolerating freedom of opinion and discussion men divide themselves into conservative and liberal organizations. It is difficult to make intelligible to an American the politics and parties of a monarchy, and yet without an insight into them one is very liable to misapprehend. The Conservative party in Spain is too content with the present, too indisposed to look far enough forward, too much wedded to tradition and prescription, and with too superstitious a devotion to monarchy; for its great leader, Canovas, in February, 1888, said in the Congress, "Monarchy is anterior and superior to the Constitution." This is perilously close to the old doctrine of the divine right of kings, that royalty never loses its right to reign.

As to the Liberal party, I have been fortunate in securing from Señor Sagasta, the Prime-minister, a paper which has the double merit of being an *ex cathedra* declaration of Liberalism, and less authoritatively a statement of Conservatism:

"The separation and difference between the Conservative and the Liberal parties takes root in the Revolution of 1868. Before that date the lines of separation of the political parties were founded neither in principles nor doctrines, public men occupying themselves with preparing for the downfall of Isabel II., which they considered indispensable to the establishment of a liberal and parliamentary *régime* in Spain. After the triumph of the Revolution of 1868 and the proclamation of the constitutional monarchy in 1869, the politics of the parties were founded on democratic principles, which are generally called individual rights. Since that date, the parties recognizing the constitutional monarchy have been formulated and defined, so that to-day they are not only perfectly distinguished, but each has a clear and definite programme. We may, therefore, classify the Conservative and Liberal parties as the two grand nuclei of political forces, around which, as occurs in England, the different tendencies of Spanish politics are grouped. In this way the Conservative party has already absorbed a great part of the Reactionaries. Those have entered into it who give more importance to religious peace than to the form of government; that is, those who are called Ultramontanes and have separated from the Carlists. Equally figures within the Conservative party, or at its side, the remnant of the old Moderate party, which was overcome in 1868. On the other hand are collected in the Liberal party those Republicans who give preference to principles over forms of government, and who strive to give efficiency to those principles by co-operation with the Liberal party. In the same attitude are found those other liberal elements the advocates of which, without being defined by a political organization, yet rely upon legal means for the triumph of their ideas and opinions. Among these may be included the Free-traders, a large part of those called Socialists, and especially the Labor party.

"At the extremes of both the great parties are two groups of real importance in the country who accept neither reforms nor legal methods of procedure, and whose reliance is upon force to accomplish the triumph of their ideals. These are the Carlists on the extreme right, and the Red Republicans on the extreme left.

"Conservatives and Liberals sustain the constitutional monarchy with equal energy, there being on this point no essential difference between the Constitutions of 1869 and 1876. Both likewise defend the rights and guarantees of individual liberty, of property, of free speech, of liberty of the press, and of establishing associations. These rights are confirmed in all the constitutions, and it is in the methods of guarantees that the difference between the parties begins. It is the aspiration of the Liberal party to commit the complete guarantee of liberty and of the electoral system to the courts of justice, while the Conservative party is inclined to exercise a guardianship over all these rights by means of administrative authorities and of ministerial power. It is in this diverse tendency that the distinction between the two parties originates and the difference of programme is born. In its platform the Liberal party affirms the development and accomplishment not only of what are termed public liberties, which are conceded by all, but the evolution of democratic principles as proclaimed by the Revolution of 1868. Hence a series of legislative measures which have been proposed, and may be enumerated as follows:

"1. Law establishing civil marriage, the character of which is defined not only by the intervention of the State at the moment marriage is contracted, but by the absolute right of the State to regulate all its civil effects in regard both to the property and rights of the married couple and their children.

"2. Law of associations, so as to shelter this right from administrative authorities and place it under the protection of courts. The law of public meetings has been already made and has universal acceptance.

"3. Law establishing the jury system.

"4. Reform of the penal code, in order to place individual rights under the safeguard of the laws, and to regulate the liberty of the press by the combined action of the jury and the courts of justice.

"5. Law to make the guarantee against the abuses of administrative power effective by suppressing the necessity of previous authorization in order to proceed against public officials, and by giving every one the means of defence against the excesses of bureaucracy.

"6. Law enlarging the right of suffrage to the extreme limit allowed by the present condition of the culture and enlightenment of the Spanish people.

"This series of measures constitutes the programme of the Liberal party, and is now undergoing development. To this policy thus defined there naturally corresponds another series of measures of a social and administrative character, intended to give to free initiative and to individual liberty all necessary expansion as a consequence of the political programme, by intrusting the commercial life of the country to the free action of the producing classes when suitably organized.

"The Liberal party gives effect to its principles and purposes by a series of legislative and administrative regulations, which have for their object—

"1. The creation of lines of navigation.

"2. The organization of chambers of commerce at home and abroad.

"3. The creation of committees of laborers and of commissions of arbitration between capital and labor or employers and employés.

"4. The regulation of the labor of women and children.

"5. The creation of a farmers' bank.

"6. The completion of disamortization, by taking real property out of mortmain and subjecting it to the rules of private property.

"7. Revision of laws and tariffs of railways in the interests of trade.

"8. The completion of a system of communication by ordinary roads and railways, especially narrow-gauge, and by combining the principal routes with the harbors and frontiers.

"9. The establishment of various manufacturing industries.

"The Conservative party has in reality no programme confronting that of the Liberal. Its attitude is expectant and, so to speak, negative. It does not recognize the urgency of any great reforms or great legislative measures, except as concern the finances, and the organization of the military forces—

questions which belong to no party, and the solution of which appertains specially to no one political group. Given this attitude, the Conservative party is reduced to opposing the reforms of the Liberal party, but at the same time it declares itself disposed to accept them if practice demonstrates their advantage, and in any way to respect *legal* solution to which co-operation is given by an intelligent and active discussion. There is therefore no other difference than that of grade and conduct. Essential differences and opposing plans do not exist, except that in the application and the development of each of the questions indicated an opposition between the two parties may be formed at any moment. What remains to be stated will make clear this point.

"Although the two great lines of action which constitute the policy and purpose of the Liberal party have been traced, yet for a fuller understanding it is necessary to call attention to two points of view which, although not formulated, define and characterize its tendency, inasmuch as they relate to the complete and historical policy of Spain.

"One of these refers to the connection between Church and State, the basis for many years of struggles and revolutionary movements. The Liberal party, which has effected disamortization and the suppression of tithes, has lately succeeded in marching in perfect agreement with the Holy See and in restoring an understanding, for a long time disturbed, between the State and the Church. Any idea of the separation of the two powers is foreign to the policy of the Liberals. On the contrary, in the harmony of the two powers, the party seeks the complete re-establishment of peace in Spain, and a change in the opinions and conduct of the clergy, who, after having been ultramontane, now begin, under the intelligent action of Leo XIII., to separate themselves completely from politics, and to devote themselves to their purely spiritual mission. This transformation of the clergy is too beneficial for the Liberal party to ignore, or to allow it to excite any difficulty which might reproduce the worst periods of modern Spanish history.*

---

* The Spanish, English, and French journals of September,

"The other point of view relates to international policy. The Liberal party, instead of being indifferent to great questions agitating the civilized world, aspires to give Spain a place among the nations called upon and expected to exert legitimate influence in the adjustment of those questions. Her geographical position guarantees neutrality in the conflicts which may arise, but likewise offers to her the means, at a given moment, of influencing, and perhaps of deciding, such

---

1888, state that the Government makes serious complaint of the Catholic clergy in the canvass for the elections of provincial councils. The priests have advised the people to vote for Carlist and Ultramontane candidates, and the Madrid and local press urge the Government to interfere. A telegram from Madrid to the *London News* of September 10, 1888, says:

"MADRID.—The Liberals won large majorities in the provincial councils, which were re-elected yesterday, throughout the kingdom. Only a few Conservatives, and fewer Republicans, were returned. The severest struggle took place in the old Carlist districts, where the Liberals were carried with a bare majority after a most curious contest, in which the Carlists fought hard, with the assistance of the priests, who even on the day of the poll threatened the electors with ecclesiastical penalties. The Jesuits and the monks declared from the pulpits and in the streets that it was a sin against religion and the Church to vote for the Liberal candidates. Some priests even came to blows with the Liberals. The conduct of the clergy in these elections is a sufficient proof that the old spirit of intolerance and the Carlist propensities of the Basque Highlanders are not extinguished."

contests. When the different forces of Europe are nearly equally balanced, as they are to-day, Spain can throw her weight into the scale for the maintenance of peace and the protection of the interests of Humanity and Civilization."

CHAPTER XII.

Policy of the Republican Party.

This lucid statement of the Prime-minister, furnished at my request, can hardly be over-estimated as an exposition of the principles and policy of the dominant party and its most formidable competitor. The unity or design of this work, seeking to portray the progress of the principles of free government in the Peninsula, would be incomplete if the policy and measures of the Republicans, with whom I must confess my sympathy, were not brought somewhat into contrast with what has just been given. The writings and speeches of Republicans have been the source of information as to their platform.* The marked distinction as to monarchy is omitted because of the obvious

---

* Large indebtedness is due to my friend, Exc'mo Señor D. Joaquin Maria Sanroma, Counsellor of Public Instruction, Professor in the University, former Sub-Secretary in the Foreign Office, and author of several valuable books.

antagonism in form and essence between a monarchy and a republic. Some unfortunate disagreements among Republicans cause a segregation into at least three factions. Treating Republicans as a unit, and passing over, except incidentally, their want of coincidence of opinion on some measures of administration, the separation from Liberals, to whom they are most closely related, may be classified under several heads.

(*a*) The political question. Apart from the form of government, there are such subjects as the composition of the Legislature, suffrage, the press, and the right of meeting. Some Republicans do not concede the necessity of two branches of the Legislature (as some do not in England), but all hold that the Senate, if it exist, should not be hereditary, nor by appointment of the Crown, nor based on wealth, but should be representative of provinces, as in the United States, or of great social interests. Republicans demand the immediate establishment of universal suffrage, without any other limitation than sex, age, criminality, etc.

Public opinion, to be safe, or consistent with a proper administration, should have some regular and judicious means of acting directly and peaceably on the machine of government and bearing on the public counsels. In the present condition of society, no government can be prosperous or permanent which does not provide for expressing and giving effect to the general sense of the people.

The Conservatives, now biding their time, and giving a *quasi* or negative support to the Liberal Government, would at once organize all their forces for its overthrow if Sagasta were seriously to insist upon the extension of the franchise. Martinez Campos, late Captain-general of Madrid, mentioned as leading the movement to bring Alfonso to the throne, is a bitter opponent of democracy, and has frankly told Sagasta that he will oppose any measures that can lead to universal suffrage.

In Spain the Ministry of the day carries the elections, and the more easily as it deals with restricted suffrage. The franchise is now confined, with certain exceptions, to Spaniards who have the three conditions of age (twenty-five years), of domicile, which involves the difficulty of getting on the register, and of a minimum contribution of twenty-five pesetas ($5) as real property tax, or double that amount as "industrial tax." Republicans seek to get rid of this last limitation, and hence demand a return to the Constitution of 1869. The exceptions have an aristocratic or class tinge. Suffrage is given to all members of academies and ecclesiastical chapters, to all parish priests and their curates, to all civil servants whose pay is over four hundred dollars a year, to all pensioners (and their name is legion), and to all painters or sculptors who have obtained a first or second class medal. Politicians are expert in the care of the registers, and the object is not to increase the list, but to keep out as many voters as possible. Madrid has 400,000 inhabitants or more. Under the old Constitution the voters should number 70,000 or 80,000. The actual register is about 12,000, a large number of whom are public functionaries or on the civil list. In the towns and rural districts the elections are a farce, and hence the desire of the Republicans for a change of the law. Monarchists impose restrictions on liberty of the press so as to exempt the royal family from criticism or censure. Republicans are content with the restrictions of the penal code, and regard the freedom of the press as essential to liberty, but subject always to considerations of public tranquillity and order.

(b) Administrative reforms, such as Communes or Districts, Army, Finance, etc. Monarchists favor very little the policy of decentralization, and aim at the concentration of power under the ægis of supreme central authorities. Republicans would discourage the centrifugal tendencies by establishing local liberties, leaving to free popular election all local officers, and giving to them the decision of all affairs pertaining exclusively to the district. They favor popular government in local matters, would give to the people a direct interest in politics and in administration, and seek something like our municipal or township governments, where local patriotism would be enkindled, the discipline of self-government acquired, and the people would be knit together in daily relations, not as common subjects but as fellow-citizens, and would find themselves to be to the State not mere ciphers but intelligent entities. Spain has no Irish question. Local agitations and demands do not disturb national repose. Still, the experience of modern governments and the philosophy of civics show the educatory, training value of local organizations. There is manifest need for the play of national and provincial patriotism, for distribution of political authority, for habits of organization, for a training which informs and raises men in intelligent, self-regulated, legal freedom. As to the army, the difference practically seems not to be great, as all parties apparently favor, or yield to, national armament, compulsory service, preparedness for war, and are dazzled by military glory. All Spaniards sigh for the return of the position of power that their country had under Charles and Philip, and would have it to play some other part than that of peninsular neutrality and isolation in the great European questions which portend early and wide-reaching results. The strain of universal military service under which the Eastern Continent groans may be favorable to dynasties and the ambition of officers, but is fatal to the prosperity and liberties of the masses. It gives the privilege, little enviable, of being among the nations most heavily indebted. *Pronunciamientos*, an untranslatable word, are uniquely Spanish, and are fostered by the deplorable military organization. The army has about 75,000 men in active service, with more generals than France or Germany. The last publication gives seven effective captains-general, six general officers about the person of the King, seventy-six lieutenants-general, 395 brigadiers, 2800 field-officers, and about 17,500 officers of lower grade. As a security against escape from military service, every Spaniard is required to provide himself with a *cédula*, an official certification of his birth and residence, and without which he may be arrested in passing out of the country, or from one province to another. Financial questions, as in most countries, are controlled by the selfish and readily combining few, and the burdens in Spain, as elsewhere, are unequally distributed. On industrial questions no very distinct line of demarcation between parties can be drawn, although Spain is an inviting field for the political economist, offering a wide scope for errors to be avoided and for experimental plans of reform and amelioration.

The Conservatives, as a rule, are united in favor of traditional restriction on trade, while among Liberals and Republicans are to be found partisans of free exchange and fierce protectionists. Ignorance of economic questions, of the fundamental ideas of production, distribution, and exchange, is widespread.

(*c*) A clearer divergence exists as to the magistrature and judicial procedure. During the session of the Cortes, 1887–88, oral procedure and jury trial have been discussed in the Senate as a Government measure and passed, but it has been antagonized by the Conservatives, and drags its slow length along, the Government fearing the issue.* Republicans advocate jury trials, and would not make the selection of a jury to rest on a feudatory basis, but make all who can read and write eligible to the service. Nor would they exclude political trials from the jury,

---

* In January, 1888, at a dinner given by the Papal Nuncio, speaking to the Minister of Justice of a naturalized American citizen imprisoned and not furnished with specific charges, I suggested the need of the right of *habeas corpus* as obtains in England and the United States, and he replied, "Spain moves calmly."

regarding such cases as appropriately cognizable by such tribunals.

(*d*) On the colonial question the difference is very wide, and properly so; for the colonial system is wasteful, corrupt, and irresponsible.* Deputies said in the Cortes in 1872, " Cuba is sunk under an inundation of abuses, and a *plus ultra* is impossible unless indeed the extermination of the whole islanders be decreed;" "Cuba is groaning under the scourge of arbitrary power; there is no law, no code, no constitution;" "Send back the twelve thousand vultures who are devouring Cuba." Of Porto Rico Froude says, " The island is a nest of squalor, misery, vice, and disease;" and of Cuba, "the Government is unimaginably corrupt, and the fiscal policy oppressive and ruinous." There have been some reforms of administration in the re-

---

* Spain holds Cuba, Porto Rico, the Philippine, Sooloo, Marianne, and Caroline islands, Ceuta, and some other possessions in Africa. To these she clings with tenacity, and the more firmly as her vast territories have so completely slipped from her grasp. Gibraltar is a perpetual sore and insult, and in the modern scramble over, and arbitrary partition of, Africa, Spain has so far been able to acquire but sterile possessions or doubtful claims, which she retains only by tolerance of other powers.

mote dependencies; but what Gladstone said in May, 1887, of England and Ireland is, names being changed, equally descriptive of Spain and Cuba. "Every horror and every shame that could disgrace the relations between a strong country and a weak one is written upon almost every page of our dealings with Ireland." The Colonies are now largely subordinate to military authority. Senators and deputies are chosen under the eye of the Government, municipalities are under metropolitan control, and everything is regulated by the central power. Republicans are autonomists, and would concede home-rule or colonial legislatures, subject to the unquestionable supremacy of the Peninsular Government. They would have an elective, popular, and representative authority in the islands, with large powers, and with control over things that affect daily life, so as to bring responsibility and a training in politics to the door of the dweller in the cottage. What Lord Salisbury lately said is equally applicable to Spain and her colonies, and in a wider sense than the Prime-minister intended: "The object of local government is to place in the hands of the people of the locality the power hitherto exercised by departments in London—departments ... too far separated, socially and locally, from those with whom they have to deal to be able to determine the measures which will be most acceptable and useful to the locality."*

(*e*) On the religious question, as might be expected, the difference is radical. Article XI., previously quoted, is deceptive, and, supplemented by the penal code, is a snare to enmesh the unwary. A Protestant school

---

* Mr. Waddington, the French ambassador in London, in the *Nineteenth Century* for June, gives an instructive article on local government in France. By the organic law of 1871 the country is divided into departments, each department into *arrondissements*, and each *arrondissement* into cantons. The canton, an aggregate of rural *communes*, or parishes, is the electoral unit for the election of the *conseil général*, a body " whose duties are largely concerned with the management and maintenance of the wonderful net-work of roads which is spread all over France, and to which each canton sends a member chosen by universal suffrage.... The electors know perfectly well the candidates who canvass their votes, and therefore only choose men who live among them, and whom they can trust; and that is the reason why the *conseils généraux*, as a whole, are more conservative, more steady than the parliamentary representatives returned by the same electors; consequently, although parliamentary institutions are often violently attacked in France, no one ever thinks of calling in question the efficacy of the *conseils généraux*."

or church, or a Hebrew synagogue, may be opened by a Spaniard, but he would be liable to persecution under frivolous pretexts. To reply by lecture or in print to a personal attack made from a pulpit, to speak disrespectfully of dogma or clergy, to put up a sign on the street or ring a bell advertising worship, to march as a Sunday-school procession with banners or music through a street, would make the persons so offending liable to the penalties of the law. Clericalism is a potential factor in Spain, and the liberty of worship, in the rural districts and villages remote from the capital and large cities, is unquestionably dependent upon the politics, the whims, the prejudices of the magistrates, the priests, and the people. Republicans favor freedom of worship, full and adequate, without evasions, without discriminations, without State support of Church. Instead of a timid, half-furtive inscription of Catholic marriage in the civil register, they would re-establish civil marriage as it existed during the revolutionary period. The Government had reformed the bigotry and despotism of the old law, and allowed validated marriages before a civil magistrate;

but when Alfonso became king he nullified them by a royal decree. The present Liberal Government has made a scary effort to get back to civil marriage, but it is hampered by a concordat with the Pope, and objection is made in the Vatican to a measure pending in the Cortes. Nothing could better illustrate the mediæval bondage of Spain, the want of real national independence, the evils of Church and State alliance. This assumption, if recognized, would vest the hegemony of Spain, of Europe, of all civil governments, in the Pope or Church of Rome. As to the basal question of the relation between Spain and the Roman Catholic Church, of which the concordat is the last expression, the Republicans would make a more liberal concordat, or, better still, would place the Roman Catholic and the other Churches on the same footing, and proclaim the independence of Church and State with sufficient guarantees against the encroachments of the so-called spiritual power.

CHAPTER XIII.

Reforms Needed.—Hope for the Future.

IN addition to reforms contemplated by Liberals and Republicans there are some others which demand immediate and thorough adoption.

(*a*) The rigid prohibition of bull-fights. This national *fiesta*, disgusting, demoralizing, cruel, brutal, bloody, is probably the most distinctive characteristic of Spain. It begins on Easter Sunday, is kept up on Sabbaths and whenever a special religious *función* is to be performed, is strangely popular, and a serious effort to suppress, by Church and Government combined, would provoke violent and revolutionary opposition. When Joseph Bonaparte arrived in Madrid, the populace, indifferent as to rulers, was much absorbed in the question whether he would grant or suppress the bull-fight.

(*b*) The abolition of lotteries. Such expedients are thinly disguised gambling, and sap the foundations of good morals. To their pernicious influence may probably be traced the fact that nearly all card-playing by men and women in Spain is connected with wagers of money. Buying lottery tickets is almost universal, from street beggar to highest official. The feverish excitement engendered causes work to be neglected, encourages aimless idleness, and deludes people with the expectations of fortunes without labor. Speculation is encouraged, honest toil is dishonored, and there is dependence for living on chance instead of on industry and frugality. The State legalizes, monopolizes, manages, and controls, and relies upon lotteries as a source of revenue in disregard of the law of economics. The budget for 1887-88 estimates the receipts from lotteries at $15,400,000. This inclusion of receipts is a delusive attempt to get something for nothing. The wealth of a State is productive labor, and the fewer the number of unproductive laborers, and the more productive the industry, the greater will be the wealth.

A fiscal reform, not remotely foreign to the abolition of lotteries, would be to reorganize the loose system of tax collection and get rid of the chronic deficits, of which in the last three years there have been 108, 91, and 77 millions of pesetas respectively. A better devised and regulated system of taxation, more responsibility in better-paid officials, exposure and punishment of thinly disguised and flagrant revenue frauds, withdrawing salaries and pensions from useless officials, economy and honesty in expenditures, would soon make possible a more favorable balance-sheet. Secretary Manning said a treasury surplus was a standing proof of bad finance. Mr. Gladstone said some people appear to suppose that public economy is the sole principle of sound finance. It is a matter of first importance, but not the only principle. The first of these principles is that the revenue and expenditure should balance together year by year. Each successive head of the Treasury Department resorts to all sorts of financial makeshifts and juggleries to "square the circle," and pay debts with new promises, or get revenue where the rapacity and follies of the Government prevent the accumulation and use of capital. When will people learn the lesson that bad government, unjust laws, favoritism to particular interests, pensioners upon labor, repression of trade, are hinderances to production and wealth?

(c) A thorough, well-organized, well-supervised, well-sustained system of public schools, controlled by the Government, in which all children between eight and eighteen should receive gratuitous instruction from competent, well-trained, and well-paid teachers. Diligent efforts to obtain late and accurate educational statistics have proved futile. By the census of 1877, of the population above twelve years of age sixty per cent. could not read. The illiteracy of the women is appalling, for they made up nearly two-thirds of this dark percentage.

Spain must learn lessons from her former colonies, where "vast provinces, which had languished for centuries under the leaden sway of a stationary system," have been revivified by the influences of an active civilization. Freedom of worship, of speech, of the press, trial by jury, representative government, "association in equality," will lift up countries and peoples. The causes preventive of greater improvement in powers and condition, of good government, are moral rather than political. Well-defined constitutional liberties are needed, but paper definitions and guarantees are inadequate to create a higher standard of political morals, and to free Spain of the intolerable burdens which repress the energies and retard the growth of a people who have made sublime exhibitions, against fatal odds, to assert national independence and personal liberty. The administration is fearfully corrupt, or, what is nearly tantamount, the people have lost confidence in the integrity of their public men, and office is almost universally regarded as the coveted means and the favoring opportunity for making money. Honest labor for support is discouraged by Government lotteries, by civil allowances, by the general desire for official place and stipend. Spaniards have excessive self-complacency and self-sufficiency, live and rejoice in an illusion that they constitute a superior race of the best blood, and they nourish themselves on reminiscences of the past, on the immortal deeds of a glorious ancestry. Individuality of character needs developing, for the structure of society and habits of government are peculiarly unfitted to that attainment. Women need to be educated and lifted out of Moorish suspicions and subordination. Division of society into artificial classes and unmanly subservience to the titled need to be reformed in law, in manners, and in habits of thought. An open Bible is the grand desideratum.

With all the undoubted drawbacks the drift in Spain is not strong, not consistent, but hopefully towards constitutional principles, promoting the general good while conserving individual rights.* Under the tuition and guidance of Liberals and Republicans the advance must be towards democratic government, towards the recognition of that "perfect liberty which is bounded only by the equal liberty of every other." Free government is not Minerva-born, not the improvisation of an inspired moment or man, not usually definitely projected, but is a slow and gradual development, moulded step by step, year by year, out of occurring exigen-

---

* In 1887 I heard Castelar make in the Cortes a significant and triumphant reference to the fact that twenty years before, the President of the Congress, the Prime-minister, and himself were under sentence of death for their Liberal opinions.

cies and increasing popular insight and courage. Great crises, in which men's minds are deeply and roughly stirred, are often helpful, for they jostle men from their stagnancy, produce disdain of authority and boldness of thinking, and awaken inquiry and doubt as to things and opinions long uninquiringly accepted. In periods of agitation, human society and human intellect make great advances. Men begin to speculate and reason, and their former idols, the gods of their worship, tumble, like Dagon, to the ground. They see the dark contrast between conduct and professions, the union of immorality and hypocrisy with ostentatious religion, the falseness of the "divinity that doth hedge a king," and at once they demand to see and examine for themselves the patents of nobility, the alleged commissions from heaven to rule over bodies, minds, and consciences of men. The multitude, so aroused, cannot help challenging institutions and dogmas, however hoary with age or sanctioned by prescription, and Thought expresses itself in protest and in overthrow of aristocracy, priestcraft, and monarchy. Blind reverence gives way to honest scepticism and wise unbelief, and the foundations on which Prerogative rears its lordly and exclusive pretensions are undermined. It was most fortunate that behind the Constitution of the United States, anterior to the Federal Union, as generative, formative, and "a school-master," lay all the struggles and achievements of our English ancestors, our colonial history, the teachings of liberty-loving statesmen and philosophers, and, above all, the increasingly comprehended doctrines of the New Testament.

APPENDIX A.

Sketches of Fernando, Leopold, Duke of Montpensier, and Amadeo.

The theory of hereditary royalty, exclusion of the wisdom of the nation in the selection of the Executive, confinement of the crown to elect families, is that royal persons are carefully trained for sovereignty, and are therefore better prepared for solving or understanding great political problems. As helping to test the theory and to elucidate the historical events which have been given as links in the chain of the progress of political ideas, brief summaries are presented of the biographies of the men who were most prominent in connection with the vacant throne.

Augusto Francisco Antonio Fernando, Duke of Saxe-Coburg-Gotha, was born in 1816, and in 1836 married Dona Maria II., Queen of Portugal, by whom he had five sons and two daughters. On the birth of the eldest son, the present king of Portugal, he received the title of King Consort, and several times during his life acted as regent of the kingdom. He acquired general esteem by the liberality of his views, a remarkable aptitude for government, and his successful efforts to maintain tranquillity in the kingdom. In 1863 he was offered the throne of Greece, which he declined. His refusal to accept the Spanish crown has been mentioned. As justifying these declinations, and, perhaps, to relieve himself of further importunities, he made public the morganatic marriage which he had contracted with an American prima donna, whose maiden name was Louise Hentzler. She was born in Boston, and was the daughter of a respectable citizen, a German tailor. For a while she sang in the choir of King's Chapel, but some wealthy members of that congregation subscribed money and sent her to Europe to acquire a more thorough musical education. She connected herself with an opera troupe, and Ferdinand, seeing her, was fascinated, and they were married. Husband and wife lived happily together. Through her efforts and taste, with his cheerful co-operation, a palace at Cintra, purchased for $3000, was beautified and enriched, and became the attractive place of Portugal. She has had much trouble, with some litigation, because of the hostility of the Portuguese to a marriage outside of royal blood; but she is, nevertheless, a woman of rare accomplishments, and has deported herself in a most exemplary manner. Fernando was an enlightened prince, a painter and engraver of considerable merit, the President of the Royal Academy of Science in Lisbon, and died near the end of 1885, much lamented.

LEOPOLD, Prince of Hohenzollern, brother of the King of Roumania, was born September 22, 1835, and on September 12, 1861, married the Infanta Antonia, daughter of the above-mentioned Fernando, king of Portugal. Prim, in his conference with Mercièr, the French ambassador, when the election of Leopold as king of Spain was announced, said, "He is a Catholic, of royal lineage, thirty-five years old, of good bearing, has two sons, and, what will predispose much in his favor, is married to a Portuguese princess." During the discussion of his candidature at Berlin, it was said by the Liberals that his accession was doubtful, but if he shall become king, the Spaniards will not have made a bad choice. In the Franco-Prussian war he was attached to the staff of the King; now he is lieutenant-general of infantry in the German army. He finds less charm in the military life than in the study of the sciences. In 1887, the prince, in going to and returning from Portugal, passed through Madrid and spent several days in visiting places of interest. He had an audience of the Queen, and their emotions as they thought of what might have been were doubtless very peculiar. The prince was strictly *incog.*, and his coming and going were known only to a very few persons. To a member of the German Legation he said he was very glad that he was not the king of Spain.

The DUKE OF MONTPENSIER, youngest son of Louis Philippe, the last king of France, was born July 21, 1824. When Queen Isabella was married at the palace, October 10, 1846, at the same time and place occurred the marriage of the duke to the sister of the Queen, Infanta Luisa. It has been often charged that the duke brought about the marriage of the Queen, a frail, unhealthy girl, to an imbecile cousin, in the confident expectation of her early and childless death, and of the consequent succession of his wife to the throne. The marriages excited an angry diplomatic controversy; and Great Britain, through Mr. Bulwer, her Minister, protested against the projected marriage of the Infanta to the duke as a violation of the Treaty of Utrecht (1713), which declared as a principle of European policy that the kingdoms of France and Spain should never be united under one sceptre, and as seriously affecting the future relations between Great Britain and Spain. Lord Palmerston said that "the decision of the king of the French that the Duke of Montpensier should *not* be a candidate for the hand of the Queen of Spain . . . was the result of the sense which the King spontaneously entertained of what was due by France to the faith of the transactions of the Treaty of Utrecht and to the just value attached by other States to the maintenance of the balance of power in Europe."

Guizot boasted to the French Chambers that the Spanish marriages constituted the first great thing France had accomplished single-handed since 1830. Palmerston, annoyed at his discomfiture, denounced them as acts of bad faith and political aggrandizement. These statesmen, looking after the interests of dynasties, did not foresee that very early the people of both France and Spain would rise to the assertion of the grand idea that kings existed for the sake of the people, to whom belonged the right to manage their own affairs. In less than two years the House of Orleans was driven from the throne of France, in twelve years Isabella was an exile, and the Duke of Montpensier's chances for either throne were reduced almost to nothing.

A late English review (*Fortnightly*) alleges that it was through pressure brought to bear by Montpensier that Louis Philippe abdicated the throne in 1848. On October 10, 1859, the duke was made and declared an Infante of Spain. In 1870 he was active in his candidature for the crown, expended large sums of money, and employed agents to advance his ambitious views. It was to defeat him that Prim urged the election of Leopold.

One of the duke's daughters is married to the Count of Paris, the claimant of the throne of France, as uniting in his person the pretensions of both branches of the House of Bourbon, so well known in the United States as a soldier and author. Another daughter, Mercedes, was the first wife of Alfonso XII. A granddaughter, Amélie, daughter of Comte' de Paris, was married in 1886 to the Duke of Braganza, Crown Prince of Portugal; and one of the current and prejudicial *on dits* in Spain is that the duke prevented a union between the Crown Prince and the Infanta Eulalia in order to secure her hand for his son, the Prince Antoine. By virtue of the renunciation at the Peace of Utrecht,

Appendix A. 141

made by the Duke of Orleans of that day, "all his descendants are excluded and incapacitated from succeeding to the throne of Spain," and therefore the descendants of the Duke of Montpensier would be excluded. Such have been the mutations in governments, what elicited an earnest remonstrance in 1846 failed to awaken even a curious comment in 1886.

The duke is a tall, graceful, fine-looking gentleman, cordial and familiar in his manners, pleasant and plausible in conversation, and impressive in general demeanor. He has much personal courage and determination, has killed one man in a duel, as related in Hay's "Castilian Days," and is tinged, probably as the result of his checkered and agitated life, with cynicism and distrust of his kind. He has a fine palace in Seville, San Elmo, which many Americans have visited, and a country home near San Lucar. He has an unenviable reputation for intrigue, and in 1888 the Government made to him a remonstrance in connection with the assemblage of some supposed French conspirators at his house.

Distrusting the account of his conduct and motives given in Spanish books, I addressed a note to him at the instance of the Count and Countess of Paris, and received a courteous reply, which it is but just to the duke I should publish.

"San Lucar de Barrameda,
21 *Avril*, '88.

"Monsieur le Ministre,—J'ai été extrêmement touché de l'aimable pensée que vous a inspiré en m'écrivant votre lettre de 22 Avril et de votre desir de rétablir la justice et la verité en ce qui me concerne dans le livre que vous écrivez sur l'Espagne. Mais je ne puis écrire le récit dont vous me parlez; j'ai été poursuivi à propos de mon mariage en 1846 et des Révolutions qui ont eu lieu en Espagne en 1856 et 1868 et années suivantes par des calomnies tellement iniques et tellement infames que j'ai pris la ferme résolution de ne leur répondre que par le silence du mépris. Les faits existent; ma conscience est tranquille; je crois n'avoir obeii dans ma vie agitée qu'aux lois de l'honneur et du devoir.

"Je ne puis rien dire de plus et il ne me reste qu'à vous remercier de tout cœur de ce que vous me dites a ce sujèt et de vous serrer le main en restant toujours

"Votre très affectionné,
"Antoine d'Orléans."

Amadeo, Duke of Aosta, Prince of Savoy, son of Victor Emmanuel, King of Italy, was born May 30, 1845. He is an amiable, gentlemanly person, a lover of sport, a good horseman, disinclined to study, indifferent to matters of government, and was almost coerced by his father to accept the crown. Those who knew him in Italy vaunted without stint the excellence of his family relations as in striking contrast with

those of the Bourbons, and spoke of him as a
good father and a loyal husband. He was not
of those of vigorous determination and strong
convictions who change their times, and he
never took the initiative in politics. Of all
rôles he preferred that of the bourgeois king,
and was often alone on the streets with stick in
hand and followed by his dog. On the day of
his arrival in Madrid he went alone to see Prim,
who was lingering in *articulo mortis* from the
assassins' attack of a few days previous. Zorrilla
speaks of him affectionately as being brave,
modest, generous, accessible to everybody, as
polite in his salutations of workmen as of the
aristocracy, indifferent to pomp and official ceremony,
and having all the elements of popularity.
When he renounced the crown, believing
that all his efforts would be sterile, he retired
with the Queen and infant child to Portugal,
where his sister was queen. Returning to Italy
and surrendering the title of king, the Italian
Parliament voted an annual allowance of 400,-
000 francs, and Victor Emmanuel named him
lieutenant-general in the army, a position which
he still holds. The princess whom he had married
in 1867 died at San Remo in 1876, and left
three sons. After a widowhood of twelve years
he married, on September 11th, at Turin, with

magnificent parade and ceremonial, his niece, the Princess Marie Létitia Bonaparte, daughter of his eldest sister, Princess Clotilde, who in 1859 was married to Prince Jerome Bonaparte. This marriage of the duke makes some queer relationships. The princess is sister-in-law to her own mother, step-mother to one set of cousins, and aunt to the remainder, while the duke becomes son-in-law to his sister, nephew to his brother, and brother-in-law to his nephews. The Bonaparte family, although as a reigning dynasty its pretensions are ridiculous, is not excluded from the charmed circle, the elect few, which European royalty reserves for its marriages—and the duke in his selection has not excluded himself from the register of "the blooded and the legitimate." A dispensation for a marriage within the prohibited degrees, prohibited by human and divine law, the Pope has granted with his blessing. Such privileges are seldom accorded except to royalty.

The abdication of a king, young and not personally objectionable, is so unusual that perhaps something in addition to what has been stated may be of interest and throw light on the extraordinary occurrence. It is well known that Victor Emmanuel overcame the reluctance of his son to accept the Spanish crown; for, having entered upon a struggle with the Pope, he deemed an alliance with a Latin and Catholic country of great advantage to Italy.

The prejudice against and opposition to Amadeo made it apparent that he was not taking a firm hold in Spain, and that his reign at best was precarious. This caused among the various political parties conspiracies against the monarchy. A combination of endangered interests was also formed to effect his overthrow. Among the intrigues which disgusted the King and engendered the thought of surrendering the crown was a scheme for the independence of Cuba, which, it was thought, with the adverse sentiment existing in the Peninsula, could not be brought about except amid the disorders and convulsions which would attend an abdication. The demand for reforms in Porto Rico, including immediate abolition of slavery, which were pressed by many leading men, threw the Cortes into a fierce excitement, and the Reactionaries were not timid in hinting at the accession of the young Prince Alfonso. The vast interests which had grown into being and had profited by despotism and slavery in Cuba and Porto Rico united with any faction to postpone emancipation. When the Ministry determined to make colonial reform a Government measure, a league of all the elements of opposition, called "A League to defend the National Domain," was formed. As the reforms included some municipal liberty as well as emancipation, it was alleged that the concession of self-government to the Colonies would involve the loss of the American possessions. The cry for the integrity of the kingdom was seductive, and had the formidable combination of newspapers, which, well supplied with money, stimulated the national pride and evoked the national hostility to foreigners by charging that there was between the Cabinet and the United States a compact degrading to Spanish honor and dangerous to national interests. The League made a formal demand upon the King for his interposition. When he declined, the dynasty became the object of imbittered attack. Strenuous efforts were made to produce insubordination in the army. Hidalgo, an officer of the artillery corps, composed mainly of aristocrats and Conservatives, had taken part in the insurrection of 1866, the prelude to the revolution of 1868, and under the revolutionary government had been made general. Hidalgo, being assigned to the command of a province in the north (he had had previously commands in Cuba and Catalonia), the artillery corps would not consent to his command of them, and asked to be retired. To punish this indiscipline, the Government accepted the resignations, resolved to suppress the corps, and submitted a decree to the King for that purpose. He asked time for reflection. The Ministry feared that this boded a refusal and their consequent resignation, and they determined to secure his approval. The League and such notable men as Topete and Duke De la Torre besought the King to undo the acts of his Ministers, which had given so much dissatisfaction to the army, and promised the loyal troops for his defence in the event of a conflict, which no one doubted if he declined to sign. As the King was impressed by these representations, the Ministers adroitly secured, through an interpellation, the submission of the matter to Congress, and obtained approbation of their proceedings. This conduct of the Ministry, in conspiring to fetter the action of the sovereign and make him dependent on them, is said to be in antagonism to the theory of the Government and traitorous to the King, whose ministers they were.* However that may be, the King, wounded in his dignity by this vote of confidence in his Ministers, was reduced to a terrible alternative. To sign,

---

* Lieber's Life and Letters, p. 107.

or not to sign, meant a bloody struggle; so he summoned the Ministry and presented his abdication. If he had accepted the advice of either party he would probably have shared the fate of Louis XVI. of France, or of Maximilian in Mexico. Spain should ever be grateful to him for saving her from the horrors of a frightful civil war. In the letter to the Chamber, from which an extract has been given, he deplored the infatuation of Spaniards, who "with sword and pen and speech aggravated and perpetuated the troubles of the nation. . . . Amid the confused, appalling, contradictory clamor of contestants, amid so many and such widely opposed manifestations of public opinion, it is impossible to choose the right, and still more impossible to find a remedy for such vast evils." This explanation of the cause of the abdication would be incomplete if the opinion of Manuel Ruiz Zorrilla, the Prime-minister at the time, were not given. In the little book, "A sus Amigos y a sus Adversarios," published in 1877, a copy of which was sent me by the author, he said that he did not know and never expected to know why the King renounced the throne. Certainly, no prince ever cared less for the gewgaws and attractions of royalty, or resigned a diadem more cheerfully and philosophically.

When he discovered that his reign was unsatisfactory, he stepped down from the throne without parade and with calm dignity. Although fifteen years have elapsed, there is no evidence that he has ever regretted his abdication, nor has one word of asperity or bitterness escaped his lips, notwithstanding the affronts and vexations he endured.

APPENDIX B.

Sketches of Christina, Isabel, Alfonso XII., the Infantas, the Queen Regent, and Alfonso XIII.

ROYAL FAMILY SINCE 1833.—When Ferdinand VII. died in 1833, his widow, Christina, a sister of a king of Naples, became regent and guardian of the children, having been so constituted by the will of the King. In 1836, as has been recited, she was compelled, at La Granja, by the soldiers to restore the Constitution of 1812, which had been violently put down, fourteen years before, by a French armed intervention. Losing all influence in the management of public affairs, she soon resigned the regency and gave herself up to unworthy passions. With her paramour she contracted an illicit marriage, which by papal absolution and authorization was afterwards validated. In 1841 she made a pilgrimage to Rome, and was cleansed of her sins and readmitted to the bosom of the Church. By her bad conduct she was temporarily estranged from her legitimate offspring, whom she cruelly neglected. Her avarice was remorseless. She dissipated the Crown property, stripped the pal-

Appendix B.

ace of valuables, sent them away or converted them into money, and made the royal residence a house of penury. Jewellery and plate disappeared, and the baptismal robe of Isabella II. was offered for sale to the American Minister. Her depraved taste substituted vulgar parvenus for refined society.

In consequence of the disorganized condition of the country, the Ayuntamiento of Madrid assumed power as the Supreme Junta of the kingdom, and undertook to dictate conditions to the Queen. The corporations of the principal cities followed the example of the capital and threw off allegiance to the Queen's Government, which became powerless. Yielding to the exactions of the Revolutionary party, Christina invested General Espartero, President of the Council, with authority to form a Ministry. Abandoning the country, she went to France, her departure causing no regret, as her errors and weaknesses had made her unpopular. It was currently reported at the time of her retirement from the Spanish throne that she had a clear fortune of from six to eight millions of dollars.

In 1844 she was again at the palace, exerting much influence over her daughter, whom she took to the baths for her health. In 1845 she had a diplomatic intrigue at Rome, in which the Spanish Minister, acting under secret instructions from her, took the Government by surprise, and there was played a game, a distinguished contemporary being judge, "in which it was doubtful whether the woman and the priest would not be an overmatch for Narvaez, the bold and wary soldier." In 1846, through the exertions of Christina and the priests, Narvaez was banished. By intrigues and maternal domination she was a ruling spirit in Madrid, and during O'Donnell's insurrection, when Espartero was invited to become Premier, he demanded, as a condition of acceptance, the immediate banishment of the queen-mother and the expulsion of her abettors.

The history of ISABEL is more thrilling in its facts and contrasts than a romance. Palace and poverty, homage and neglect, a queen and an exile, prediction of early death, and a hale, fat woman of near sixty years. She was born in 1830, and her father dying in 1833, left her a queen, as his rightful heir to the throne. The right was contested by Don Carlos, brother of Ferdinand, assuming the title of Don Carlos V.; and hence originated Carlism, which, with its pretences of legitimacy and loyalty to the Church, has been almost to the present hour the fruitful source of disorder and conspiracy and protracted and bloody civil war. Isabel and her sister, Maria Louisa Fernanda, the wife of the Duke of Montpensier, were the only children of Ferdinand. The question of the right of succession in default of male issue assumed tangible form in the rival pretensions of the elder daughter, supported by the queen-mother and the popular party on the one side, and of Don Carlos at the head of the monks and Absolutists and many of the aristocracy on the other. Caleb Cushing, in a despatch to the Government, December 2, 1875, discusses the question with great learning and ability. "According to the ancient laws of Spain and the practice from the time of the formation of the monarchies of Castile and Leon (but not Aragon), females succeeded to the crown in default of direct male succession, and in preference to collaterals of the male sex. . . . Although Philip V. claimed through females, nevertheless, one of his earliest acts was to repeal the laws of Spain respecting succession, and to introduce instead the Salic law of France in the form of an *auto accordato,* or prerogative act. . . . With the first years of the reign of Charles IV. (1789) the Cortes petitioned him to repeal the *auto accordato* of Philip and restore the immemorial custom of Castile, which admitted the succession of females to the crown. The petition was unanimous, and the King assented and ordered the preparation accordingly of a *pragmatic sanction* (an old name for laws of repeal) to that effect, but ordered further that the whole proceeding should remain secret and confidential until such time as the Crown in its wisdom might see fit to give publicity to the same. That time arrived in the reign of Ferdinand VII. . . . He determined to promulgate the pragmatic sanction of Charles IV., March 29, 1830. . . . That the King had the right to revive and restore the pre-existing law of Spain, a great majority of Spaniards of all classes and the most accredited jurists of Europe are of accord, the more so, seeing that the succession of females is the common law of the country, . . . and accordingly Isabel and her son Alfonso have enjoyed the recognition of all foreign powers, while none have recognized Don Carlos."* Before Ferdinand died a new Nuncio had been appointed. The Pope's brief accrediting him was, however, awaiting the signature of the Council of Castile when Ferdinand died. The Spanish Government immediately communicated to the Pope the death of the King, and the succession of Isabel II. by virtue of the

---

* Foreign Relations, 1875-76, pp. 442-445.

pragmatic sanction and the universal recognition of her subjects. Under such circumstances international law requires the renewal of the credentials of diplomatic agents. The Pope declined to recognize Isabel. His claim of interference in the political and civil affairs of a foreign independent nation caused a rupture of the political relations between Spain and Rome. The Spanish Government nominated the new bishops when vacancies occurred. The Pope objected, not because of dissatisfaction with the persons nominated, but because, not having recognized Isabel, he could not confirm her bishops and thus imply a recognition of her title. This state of affairs continued until 1848, when the Pope yielded and Isabel was recognized.*

Becoming legal queen at three years of age, during her minority there was a regency. During her tender years she was neglected by her wicked mother, and left under tutoresses and governesses who were more concerned for their selfish ends than for the public good or the welfare of the child. She did not receive the intellectual and moral training required for a sovereign. At ten years she was of slender frame and feeble health, having from her birth been

---

* Phillimore, vol. ii., p. 451.

affected with a cutaneous disease—"a sad bequest, the fruit of her father's low sensuality and dissipations." Her early death was predicted and expected. In October, 1841, a conspiracy was formed to seize and carry her to the seat of the insurrection in the Basque Provinces, and a fruitless attempt was made to abduct her from the palace. The principal conspirator was arrested, tried, condemned, and shot—a unique instance of summary punishment of a political offender.

Spain was in a deplorable condition. Factions flourished, people were turbulent, the treasury was empty, and expenditures were three years in anticipation of resources. Ephemeral Ministries could not prevent public affairs from going from bad to worse. Madrid in 1843 was in possession of 40,000 insurgents. Three rival generals were in the capital. A revolutionary government was organized in the name of Isabel II. The Cortes, on November 9th, by a vote of 193 to 16, declared her of age, and in presence of State functionaries and the diplomatic corps, assembled in the palace, the child of thirteen was so declared, and became queen *de facto* as well as *de jure*. The next year there was much speculation and criticism upon the baleful influence and bad designs of the queen-mother, who accompanied her to some medicinal baths. There were also plots and counterplots as to the marriage of Isabel, and not unnaturally, for the most ambitious might covet an alliance which would place on the throne of Ferdinand and Isabella. Some efforts to secure an alliance with the son of Carlos were made, so as to unite the two claimant families to the throne. The honor was reserved for her cousin Don Francisco de Assisi, and the marriage was celebrated in the palace on October 10, 1846, the royal consort being invested, by courtesy, with the title of King and His Majesty. It was an ill-fated and mismated match. In six months there was an undisguised coolness between king and queen, which soon ripened into estrangement from society and bed. Two attempts were made, in the course of a few years, upon the life of the young queen, one of them by a priest, who was garroted, and his body was burned by royal order. The Queen bore several children, one of whom was baptized with one hundred and nineteen names, but it did not long survive. Before the birth of the last child daily masses were said to propitiate the Holy Virgin and implore her assistance in the hour of trial. The Queen made her devotions at various altars of the different Marys, such as were supposed to exert a happy influence on such events, namely, the Maria del Leche, Maria del Bueno Partu, etc. Relics of saints, such as legs, arms, collar-bones, etc., were sent from various parts of Spain to the palace, all of which have high repute as efficacious in facilitating parturition. The press was full of detailed accounts of these proceedings, and the literature, not very elevating or edifying, was much enjoyed by the ignorant and superstitious.

In 1868 the revolution occurred, and the Queen was dethroned and fled to France. Her conjugal infidelity had much to do in awakening popular indignation. In 1870 she abdicated her right to the throne in favor of Alfonso, the Prince of the Asturias. The telegram announcing the call of Alfonso to the throne reached Paris at night. All were asleep at the hotel except the anxious mother, who, according to a sketch of Alfonso published in 1885 in the New York *Herald*, on reading the glad news, hurried, in the lightest of *négligés*, to her son's bedroom, and cried aloud, as she awoke Alfonso from a sound sleep, "See! read! You are king of Spain! Permit me, Sire, to kiss your hand as the first of your Majesty's subjects." Alfonso languidly drew his hand from under the coverlet, presented it to his mother's lips, and then turning over, fell asleep without having

Appendix B. 159

uttered a word. With the accession of Alfonso, Isabel returned to Madrid, and now she passes her time there, at Seville in the Alcazar, and at Paris. She receives from the Spanish Government an annual pension of $150,000. Suspected of intrigues for the succession and of interference with domestic affairs in the palace, she has had from the Government a gentle remonstrance as to her indiscretions, and a request not to spend too much of her time in the palace. Many persons discredit any suspicions of personal ambition. She told me she detested politics. She is not personally attractive nor very intelligent, but has cordial manners and is very amiable and generous. No one can condone her offences, but there are few persons who more merit a generous and merciful leniency. Her husband makes his separate home in Paris. Of this hero of the State policy and diplomatic intrigue, Wallis said, "There is no risk in saying that neither Lavater nor Spurzheim would hasten to select him, from outward signs, as the model of a ruler among men."

ALFONSO XII. was born November 28, 1857. When his mother was driven from the throne and Spain, and found an asylum in France, her children accompanied her. The young Prince of Asturias was sent to school at Vienna, Paris, and in England. He was a diligent student and a good scholar. When the Republic was overthrown, he was, on December 29, 1874, proclaimed king, and was accepted with much satisfaction by the army and the nation. At seventeen he entered Madrid on horseback, bareheaded, dressed as a Spanish general, and surrounded by a brilliant cavalcade. Possessed of much personal bravery, he placed himself at the head of the troops against the Carlists. On two occasions, when assassins tried to take his life, he behaved with conspicuous coolness. The latter of these attacks General Grant witnessed from the window of his hotel overlooking the Puerta del Sol. On January 23, 1878, the King married his cousin Princess Mercedes, daughter of the Duke of Montpensier. He did this against public opinion and the advice of his Ministers. It was a love-match, and deserves commendation, for few such occur in the history of royalty. She lived only five months, and her death filled the King with a sorrow which drove him into solitude from which he was with difficulty withdrawn. State reasons were pressed upon him for forming a new alliance, and on November 29, 1879, he married Maria Christina of Austria. On November 25, 1885, he died at the Palace of El Pardo, a few miles outside of Madrid. The funeral services were celebrated with great pomp and magnificence. Arriving in Madrid a few hours prior to the death, I saw him lying in state in the palace, and as special envoy represented the Government on the occasion of the funeral.

The King was intelligent and popular, and had many qualities to make him a successful ruler. His private life was not such as it should have been, and his early death was doubtless due in part to his excesses.

Infanta Dona ISABEL, sister of the King, was born December 20, 1851, and made an unfortunate marriage with Count Girgenti, brother of King Francis II., of Naples. He committed suicide three years afterwards, leaving no children. The Infanta is popular in aristocratic circles, is fond of dancing, driving, and riding on horseback, and is often seen at balls and receptions given by ambassadors and grandees of Spain. Her apartments in the palace, well fitted up, are filled with paintings, engravings, photographs, books, bric-à-brac, rare purchases, costly gifts from friends, and even her toys as a child. She is a devout Catholic, and liberal in her private charities and in her gifts to the Church. She is a woman of much intelligence, of sound discretion, of administrative capacity, a shrewd and minute observer of people and things, talks well on serious subjects, and has her full share of Spanish pride and patriotism. She has acted with much good-sense in sustaining the Queen-regent in her difficult position. Very greatly to her honor, calumny can find no ground for reproaching the purity of her life.

Infanta MARIE-DELLA-PAZ was married in 1883 to Louis Ferdinand, Prince of Bavaria. Dona EULALIA, youngest sister of the late king, is attractive and pleasant, and has hosts of friends. She was married on March 6, 1886, to her cousin Don Antoine, son of the Duke of Montpensier. At the Jubilee of Great Britain's sovereign she worthily represented the Queen-regent, and attracted much attention by her cordial manners and pleasant conversation.

MARIA CHRISTINA was born in 1858, and her father was an uncle of the present Emperor of Austria. Her mother, the Archduchess Elizabeth, is a stately, handsome woman of noble carriage, and makes a visit once a year to Madrid. Educated with her brothers, Christina has a knowledge of many branches of literature and science, and she keeps up her habits of study. She speaks easily and accurately German, French, Spanish, and English. She resigned the dignity of abbess of the Convent of

Appendix B.

Noble Ladies in Prague to become Queen of Spain. The marriage to Alfonso was witnessed by Isabel, the Infantas, the civil and ecclesiastical dignitaries, the Ministers of State, and the diplomatic corps. Thousands of people were on the streets. The balconies were hung with many-colored cloths—a scenic display for which Spain is so famous. The nuptial mass was celebrated by the Patriarch of the Indies, a cardinal, and festivals and illuminations added to the auguries of a life of happiness. Christina excluded herself from party politics and Court intrigues, and confined herself to the duties of her household. Such complete self-effacement of the queen in the wife, and such abstinence from complications with families and factions, made her incur some ill-will, and at the death of the King she had not such a hold on the nation as to awaken strong hopes of a successful reign.

Immediately on the death of Alfonso a Cabinet meeting was held, and the widow was appointed regent. The Ministry, in accordance with usage, tendered their resignations, but continued in office until their successors should be appointed. Canovas, with magnanimity, loyalty, and patriotism, advised the Queen to form a Liberal Government, that in her difficult position she might have the support of both Liberals and Conservatives. She called in Sagasta, who still remains at the head of the Government.

The Queen-regent, although inexperienced and a foreigner, has shown much tact and determination, has identified herself thoroughly with Spanish people and interests, has no friends to reward nor enemies to punish, presides every Thursday over the Council of Ministers, hears reports from the head of each Department, takes a keen and intelligent interest in home and foreign affairs; and the Ministers, individually and in the disclosures of personal friendship, give her the highest praise, and speak with surprise and gratification at her prudence and wisdom and knowledge of men.

Her Majesty has had but one grand reception, which was very brilliant, and two State dinners, one, and the more formal, of which was attended by the ex-queen, infantas, damas, grandees, the Ministry, and the chiefs of different legations and their wives. The two queens sat *vis-à-vis* at the table, and posts of precedence and honor were relative proximity on right and left to their Majesties. The *salon*, lighted with near one thousand candles, made joyous by the classical music discoursed by select military bands, by the uniforms and decorations of naval and military and civil and diplomatic guests, by the rich toilets and blazing jewellery of the ladies, and the glass and silver and gold service, brought to mind the contrast between that brilliant scene and Isabel's first dinner at the palace after she was proclaimed queen, when she was served from pewter plates, because from spoliations of her mother and others nothing better was to be had in the magnificent royal residence. The Queen receives alone in a little *salon*, and is most gracious and cordial with her visitors. Her manners are easy. Her face wears ordinarily a look of subdued sadness, but her features light up when she smiles or talks with animation. She is devoted to her children, often rides or walks with the little infantas, watches over their education, and is wrapped up in the little king. I have seen her run out of the *salon*, bring in his Majesty, hold him in her arms, kiss him on his cheeks, expose his arms and legs, and show the most fascinating interest in his health and appearance. One of the Queen's loveliest traits is the frequency with which, even on state occasions, the mother dominates the sovereign.

In a Court not unused to slander, and where, unfortunately, bad lives have prevented reproaches from being slanderous, the slightest breath of suspicion has never rested upon the fair fame of this noble woman. Once, in indignant, wifely protest against the infidelity of her royal husband, she took her two children and travelled to Austria, and there remained until induced to return by renewed marital vows, supplemented by considerations pertaining to her children and by high clerical influence.

Don Alfonso left two daughters, MARIA DE LAS MERCEDES, Princess of the Asturias, born September 11, 1880, a name given by the Queen to her first child in honor of the first wife, whose memory she knew her husband cherished, and MARIA THERESA ELIZABETH, born November 12, 1882.

In May, 1886, nearly six months after the death of Alfonso, ALFONSO XIII. was born. He was born a king—a fact unprecedented in royal annals. His birth was anticipated with eager anxiety and intense national concern. Great as Elizabeth and Maria Theresa and Catherine and Isabella the Catholic were as sovereigns, it was felt that "a man child" was necessary for the repose of Spain and the peaceful continuance of the dynasty. In Spain, with its traditional etiquette and adherence to antiquated things, the old usage of witnesses to a royal birth, to keep free from suspicion the legitimacy of the succession, is observed with scrupulous care and forethought. Several days prior to the expected birth, the diplomatic corps is formally invited by the introducer of ambassadors to witness the presentation. When the event is imminent a special notice is sent, and each chief of a mission responds promptly, dressed in full uniform. On the 17th of May, the diplomatic corps, the members of the Government, distinguished military and civil officers, assembled in a large reception-room in the palace. After an hour's waiting, Señor Sagasta, the President of the Council of Ministers, announced the happy consummation and the sex by exclaiming, "Viva el Rey." The witnesses having proceeded to a room adjoining the chamber of the Queen-regent, profert was made of the royal scion *in puris naturalibus*. There was no aureole, nor any manifestation of the divinity that is said to hedge a king, nor any evidence that he was in anywise different from the child of a peasant. The new king was received everywhere in Spain with satisfaction and cheerful declarations of support. Don Carlos, from his exile, protested against the "usurpation" of the infant king, and reasserted his rights as the legitimate sovereign, but his manifesto was impotent and unheeded. Five days afterwards the baptism occurred in the royal chapel. The grandees, the Ministers of the Crown, deputations from the Cortes and the municipality, civil, military, and clerical dignitaries, the diplomatic corps with their wives, occupied tribunes around the font, which was placed in the centre of the chapel. The prescribed mourning being suspended for that day, the men mostly wore dazzling uniforms, while the toilets of the ladies, enriched by the precious stones for which Spain is so noted, were beautiful and splendid. Such gorgeousness is rarely seen. The ceremony was not destitute of political significance; for the Pope, yielding to the request of the Queen to stand sponsor to her child, had deputed the Nuncio, Monsignor Rampolla (who is now the papal Secretary of State in Rome), to represent him. This concession was almost a death-blow to Carlism, which claims to be *par excellence* Catholic, and has derived its principal strength from Ultramontanism.

About the time of my leaving Madrid an incident occurred which illustrates the religiousness of the Queen and her acceptable conformity to a national custom. The *viaticum* was borne through the Puerta del Sol as the Queen, with her two daughters, was passing in a carriage. As soon as she saw it, ordering the coachman to stop, she dismounted and made the priest take her place, while she, with the children, followed on foot. The crowd, moved by this spectacle of humility, attended her to the church, which she entered behind the priest. After praying for some moments, her Majesty retired, and the enthusiastic multitude surrounded the carriage, unwilling to let her depart.

The luxuries of royalty are furnished to Spain at the annual cost of, for the King, $1,400,000; the Princess of Asturias, $100,000; the Infanta Isabel, $50,000; the Infanta Paz, $30,000; the Infanta Eulalia, $30,000; the Duchess of Montpensier, $50,000; the ex-Queen Isabel, $150,000; and her husband, Francisco, $60,000.

APPENDIX C.

Present Aspect of Spain.

PAPER constitutions, however perfect in theory, do not execute themselves nor make good government. There must be much behind them in the virility and self-reliance, in the intellectual alertness and moral force of the people, to secure material prosperity, high civilization, or national greatness. That Spain has suffered incalculably from bad government, civil and religious, cannot be denied. To give some information on the present condition of the country, it has seemed well to group under appropriate heads what has been obtained after diligent inquiry. Accurate and recent statistics it is almost impossible to get, and one may well be on his guard as to any statements about education, commerce, revenues, population, etc.

1. *Population.* — Many causes, ancient and modern, have prevented the increase which is seen in other parts of Europe. The expulsion of the Jews, the banishment of the Moors, chronic revolutions, civil fratricidal wars, insecurity of

person and property, have been hinderances to growth. There is no fixed period for taking the census. The last was taken in 1877, and the preceding one in 1864, and information which may lead to taxes and conscription is reluctantly given. At the last enumeration the actual population was 16,634,345; by right, 16,753,591. The latter is found by deducting immigrants not permanently domiciled and adding Spaniards who have left *animo revertendi*. Of the actual population, the males were 8,136,331 and the females 8,500,014. The percentage of deaths was reported at about 25 per 1000. The press of Madrid, on February 1, 1887, reported 50,000 deaths in Spain, the preceding year, from diphtheria. Dr. Hauser, who has published, under the auspices of the Government, a very able report, says that the deaths from cholera in 1885 amounted to 120,000. For April, 1888, in Madrid there were 1355 births and 1276 deaths.

2. *Value of Property and Amount of Taxation.*—The aggregate value of real estate can be ascertained only approximately and inferentially. In the last budget the territorial tax is assessed at $35,400,000, representing 16 per cent. of the productive value of landed property, or $220,000,000. There is no certain means of

knowing the value of the personal property. The annual taxation, as given in the last few budgets, would make it about $170,000,000. The assessment of the tax on real property is based on reports made by the municipal juntas. There is a tax on trade and industry, based on a tariff varying in proportion to the nature of the trade or industry and the number of the inhabitants of the town. An *octroi* duty—a gate-tax on consumption—is levied on salt, soap, coal, wax, vegetables and other provisions, and is collected at the gates or the borders of the town. This odious espionage tax varies according to population, the minimum being 5000, and gives to the numerous officers frequent means for oppression and peculation. Where exchange is so much fettered and government is an ingenious process of squeezing, production is much curtailed. American travellers, having had their luggage examined at the frontier custom-houses, are much surprised and grumble not a little at the annoyance of examinations as they enter every town; but it does not lie in the mouth of one of our people to complain of the custom-house grievances of other countries. Banks pay 10 per cent. on the net profits which are divided among shareholders. Railways pay a tax of 10 per cent. on all travellers' tickets, and a tax of five cents on every $500 of transportation of freight. In 1886 the taxation per capita was about $9.84. The income from customs duties by last budget was estimated at $27,000,000, and from export duty, assessed on cork and argentiferous lead, at $20,000.

The revenues of the Government are badly collected and at a loss of a ruinous percentage. It is doubtful whether half reaches the treasury, and the inadequacy for national obligations need not therefore be surprising. No one is ignorant of the corruption in the fiscal department, of the bribes and frauds; and the saying of the Spaniards that money, like oil, sticks to the fingers of those who handle it, is well justified by the collection of revenue.* Spain owes more than one thousand million of dollars, and in every annual budget a floating debt of 25 per cent. of the budget is authorized, and this is the ordinary recourse for meeting habitual deficits and extraordinary expenditures. The finance officer has "a hard road to travel" in devising

---

* Ford says, "In a land where public officers are inadequately paid, where official honesty and principle are all but unknown, a bribe is all sufficient; false returns are regularly made, and every trick resorted to to transfer revenue into the pockets of the collectors."

desperate expedients, contracting usurious loans, living from hand to mouth, and robbing Peter to pay Paul. Smuggling is a vocation in Spain, and its existence is as well known as the capital of the kingdom. "The smuggler is the type and channel of the really active principle of trade" in a large portion of the Peninsula. Making Gibraltar a free port is an act of flagrant wrong to Spain, and is a stimulus to violations of revenue laws. The Bank of Spain, established in 1872 with a capital of $50,000,000 and a privilege of enlargement to $150,000,000, the only bank of issue in the kingdom (until lately its notes were printed by the American Bank Note Company), is fast becoming the manager of the finances of the nation. It has now the monopoly of the sale of tobacco, and collects the taxes on real estate, commerce, and industry, because those taxes are mortgaged for the payment of money borrowed.

3. *Railways and other Roads.*—The old Roman roads have mostly fallen into decay and disuse. From Madrid there diverge to the principal seaport and frontier towns good highways, but intercommunications are sadly defective. In the beginning of 1885 there were 5420 miles of railway, and the principal towns are now embraced in the system. All belong to private

companies, and were built by private capital, aided by subventions from the Government on the condition that the latter shall take possession in ninety-nine years. There are generally three trains: the express, the mail, and the mixed, each of which furnishes first, second, and third class compartments for travellers. The fast train does not carry the mail; and on the general principle that nothing is to be done in a hurry, the mail which arrives at Madrid at six in the morning quietly rests until eight at night before starting on its southward journey. In 1883 there were over 10,000 miles of telegraphic lines, and in the last budget the appropriation for their management (they belong to the Government) was $1,564,800.

4. *Marriages* are allowed, with consent of parents or guardians, as soon as contracting parties are sufficiently developed. Without this consent, the minimum age for the male sex is twenty-three, and for the female twenty. Permission to contract matrimony is granted on application at the vicar's office, where the certificate of birth of both parties must be exhibited, and a fee of $12 paid. An extra charge of $30 must be paid if haste is desired by the omission of the publication of the banns during the fête days. The priest performing the cere-

mony receives $6. The expense and delay attending marriage tend to the unions without authorization which are so common in Spain. In a purely civil marriage, seldom occurring, application must be made to the municipal judge. Every canonical marriage must be entered in the Civil Register. Absolute divorces *a vinculo matrimonii* are not permitted, but separations without any privilege of remarriage can take place. The ecclesiastical courts have jurisdiction of applications for separation. Statistics are very imperfect as to the legitimacy of offspring. It is said that the average of illegitimacy in the whole country is between five and six per cent., and in Madrid twenty per cent. *El Dia* of February 1, 1887, said that during the January preceding there had been in Madrid 1402 births and 1744 deaths; of the births, 284 were illegitimate and 1118 legitimate. In April, 1888, there were 1101 legitimate and 354 illegitimate births.

Some amends are made for the obstacles thrown in the way of marriage by the abundant provision made for foundling hospitals. Most cities are supplied with these institutions for caring for the sinless children of sin. A rough English captain said they should be labelled "Adultery made easy." By law of 1822, a hospital is required for each province, divided into a compartment for lying-in women, another for infants, and a third for children under six. The law of 1849 turns over the duty of providing foundling hospitals to the provinces, and orders the provincial juntas to appoint committees of women to supervise these establishments. A nurse sits up at night to receive the children whose parents would conceal their guilt, and any examination of or interference with mothers desiring to leave their children in these hospitals is strictly forbidden.

During coverture a woman cannot have a separate estate, sign papers, make contracts, perform legal acts, without the authority of her husband, but the husband only can nullify the acts.

5. *Law of Inheritance.*—By will, heirs are of two kinds, voluntary and involuntary (*forzosos*). The latter are the direct line from testator; the former, collateral or *strangers*. The testator must leave his property to his *herederos forzosos*, or state his reasons for not so doing. The legal causes for disinherison are age of more than ten and a half years, grave insults, attempts to kill, accusation of serious crime, abandonment of testator while insane, and marriage without his consent. These reasons, so

far as applicable, will excuse one for disinheriting parents. In case of intestacy, children share equally, *per capita*, without distinction of age or sex. Grandchildren, in case of parent's death, inherit *per stirpes*. Natural children, in default of legitimate children, can inherit from their mother.

As in England, the Government derives a revenue from a tax on succession, which was estimated in the last budget at $6,200,000. These taxes on inheritance vary as to degree of relationship. By law of 1881, when the heir is legitimate and in the direct line, the tax is one per cent.; when illegitimate, two per cent. Collateral relationship is run out from second degree at four per cent. to the fifth at seven per cent., and one per cent. is added for each degree from the sixth to the tenth. Strangers must pay nine per cent. The Government levies a tax of twelve per cent. upon money left to be expended in masses for the repose of the soul of the deceased. This may be to discourage such bequests; for a shrewd observer of Spanish affairs says, "More money has been expended in masses than would have covered Spain with railroads, even on a British scale of magnificence and extravagance."

6. *Titles.*—The civil titles are duke, duchess,

marquis, marchioness, count, countess, viscount, and viscountess. These titular distinctions, dividing society into artificial classes, import no official superiority, no legal prerogatives and privileges beyond some functions, social and ceremonial, pertaining to the palace or the sovereign. By the law of 1820 and 1855, a title follows the order of succession established in the concession; but the possessor of several grandezas of Spain, or titles of Castile, may distribute them among his sons as he sees fit. A possessor of several titles may bestow some upon brothers or relatives. In every succession or bestowment, the heir or grantee must obtain a letter of confirmation, and pay a tax as follows: grandee of Spain with title of duke, marquis, or count, $2000; grandee with title of viscount, $1800; grandee with title of baron or señor, $1600; grandeza without title, $1200; title of marquis, $800; of viscount, $600; of baron or señor, $400. When there is more than one title, there is an addition of two-thirds of the tax for the second, and of one-half for the third, or any after the third. A nobleman may resign a title without its being lost or lapsed, as his son can assume it on paying the sum as required for the succession. Titles are not purchasable, but proceed from the sovereign.

7. *Civil Service.*—By laws of 1852, 1866, and 1875, elaborate arrangements are provided for examination, admission, and scales of promotion in the civil service. The theory of the diplomatic career is that men are appointed after examination, trained in foreign office or as unpaid attachés to legations, and are made and kept as ministers and ambassadors until retired upon pensions. Madrid, without commerce, without industry of any importance, with scarce an element of production, official Madrid is crowded with civil officials, with military and naval officers, with expectants waiting and scheming for the return of their party to power. The author of that clever little book, "L'Espagne telle qu'elle est," affirms that the politicians of Madrid have formed among themselves a sort of society for mutual succor, and although belonging to different parties, work harmoniously to conserve the system which enables them to get their support, directly or indirectly, from the Government. The spoils idea has fullest and most mischievous exemplification. Retiring allowances and pensions help to foster the claims to patronage and to subordinate the public good to "disgraceful struggles for the possession of office and public place." Civil officers and judges may retire after they have attained six-

ty, or be retired on reaching sixty-five, if they have had twenty years of service. An earlier retirement is allowed on proof of disability. The pay of retired civil officers after twenty years of service is forty per cent. of active pay; after twenty-five years, sixty per cent., and after thirty-five years, eighty per cent. The maximum of pay for retired civil officers is $2000. Such civil officers as entered the service before 1845 have a right, when not holding office, to half-pay. Crown ministers, who have as such held office for two years, and diplomats who have had eighteen years' service, are entitled to $1500 annually. On the civil pension list of 1877, the latest statistics published, there were 9478 men and 7614 women. The amount paid as pensions to civil and military officers and widows and orphans of such, in 1887, was $10,041,945.

8. The *Army* is raised by conscription, but exemption can be purchased on payment of $400. The peace footing is from 80,000 to 90,000 men; the war footing near 400,000. The term of service is twelve years—three active, three in active reserve, and six in the second reserve. Officers are appointed from graduates of military schools, in some cases from competitive examinations. The lieutenant-general in

command is paid per annum $5000, not in command, $3750; field-marshal, $2500; brigadier, $1800; colonel, $1600; commandant, $1100; captain, $750; lieutenant, $400; sub-lieutenant, $330; 1st sergeant, $182.50; 2d sergeant, $127.75; corporal, $100.35; soldier, $91.25. Captains-general, usually commanding a district, of which there are fourteen, receive special allowance and pay according to the dignity and importance of the post. The fixed rules for promotion are disregarded, and the most open favoritism is practised.

Private soldiers or sailors disabled in the service are cared for by the Government. They enter the Invalid Corps, and their former pay is continued. Those that have families have the choice of living outside the Home. Disabled officers can also enter the Invalid Corps, their pay being continued as in active service, and promotion every fifteen years being granted until the grade of colonel is reached. For heroic courage and military distinction additional remuneration is provided. Privates and non-commissioned officers for military distinction are rewarded with the cross for military merit, and fifty cents a month during active service; for special service in time of war, with the same cross and $1.50 a month during life; for heroic

Appendix C.

bravery, the Cross of St. Ferdinand and from $50 to $120 during life to sergeants, and $20 to $80 during life to corporals and privates. Officers are rewarded for similar services with the Cross of St. Ferdinand and during life from $75 to $300 for captains, $100 to $400 for superior officers, and from $500 to $2000 for generals. The retired pay of army and navy officers is thirty per cent. of active pay after twenty years' service, and proportionately until after forty years' service, when ninety per cent. of active pay is given. Generals are not retired, but are placed on the reserve list with from $2000 to $2500 a year, according to rank.

Frequent reference has been made in the course of this little history to the influence of the army on Spanish politics, and the use of that lever by all parties and leaders for the accomplishment of their patriotic ends or selfish ambitions. Public opinion and popular elections are too slow or too uncertain agencies for effecting political reforms, getting rid of objectionable rulers, or satisfying the greed for place and honors. Liberals, Progressives, and Conservatives have looked to and used the army for executing their plans. When palace intrigues or royal prerogatives have failed, or when the tide of events lingered too long for the impatient and impecunious, in the barracks have been found the facile and effective means of reaction and revolution. For three-quarters of a century pronunciamentos have been common in Spain, and the regular process of law has been set aside by the prompter action of soldiers. O'Donnell, Espartero and Narvaez, Castelar and Serrano, have yielded their places at the bidding of troops. Alfonso came in on bayonets, and since there have been comparative quiet and acquiescence in the improving order of things, and yet in 1883 Sagasta fell after the revolutionary surprise at Badajos. There was a military insurrection at Gerona in 1884, another at Carthagena in 1885, and still another at Madrid in 1886, which came as the first in the reign of Alfonso XIII. These were stupid, and outwardly not very serious, and yet they showed discontent and habits of indiscipline in the ranks, and a readiness on the part of officers to use the forces in their command for self-promotion or the overthrow of the Government.

The evil of political ambition in the army and of the association of political consequences with military insurrections is not easily cured. The French army has always honorably abstained from becoming an instrument of political agitation, but in Spain the army is a recognized agency for political revolutions; and the interference, instead of being punished summarily and exemplarily, is accepted as legitimate. Patriotic statesmen shrink from drastic and adequate measures for the extirpation of a chronic evil, the outgrowth of revolutions, civil wars, political usages, mock parties and elections. In 1876, 250,000 soldiers were disbanded, but the officers were retained, and by degrees even Carlist officers, from brigadier-general downward, had their army rank recognized. The vast horde of poorly paid and unemployed officers are an inviting field for political intrigue, and constitute a band of ready conspirators, who listen to the seductive voices of wily men, and dream that by the turn of the wheel they can become the future Prims of the country. The effort to reorganize the army and place it on a more economical and efficient basis, made by the present Liberal Government, has been too timid and superficial, but it has encountered from the Opposition and the army such resistance as to make its adoption almost an impossibility.

APPENDIX D.

[*From* AMERICAN MAGAZINE OF HISTORY, *April*, 1888.]

The Acquisition of Florida.

AT the beginning of this century the relations of the United States with foreign powers were much complicated. At no other period of our history have so many and such difficult questions of an international character been presented for discussion and settlement. The wisdom and firmness and potential influence of Washington, the strong republican convictions of Adams, the large and varied ability of Jefferson, Madison, and a number of eminent diplomatists, the patriotism and integrity of all, were demanded in full to adjust our new republic to her rightful position in the family of nations. International jurisprudence was in an unsettled condition. It has very slowly acquired the certainty and precision now recognized by government courts and by treatises on the Law of Nations. In fact, no nation since 1789 has contributed more to the settling of the

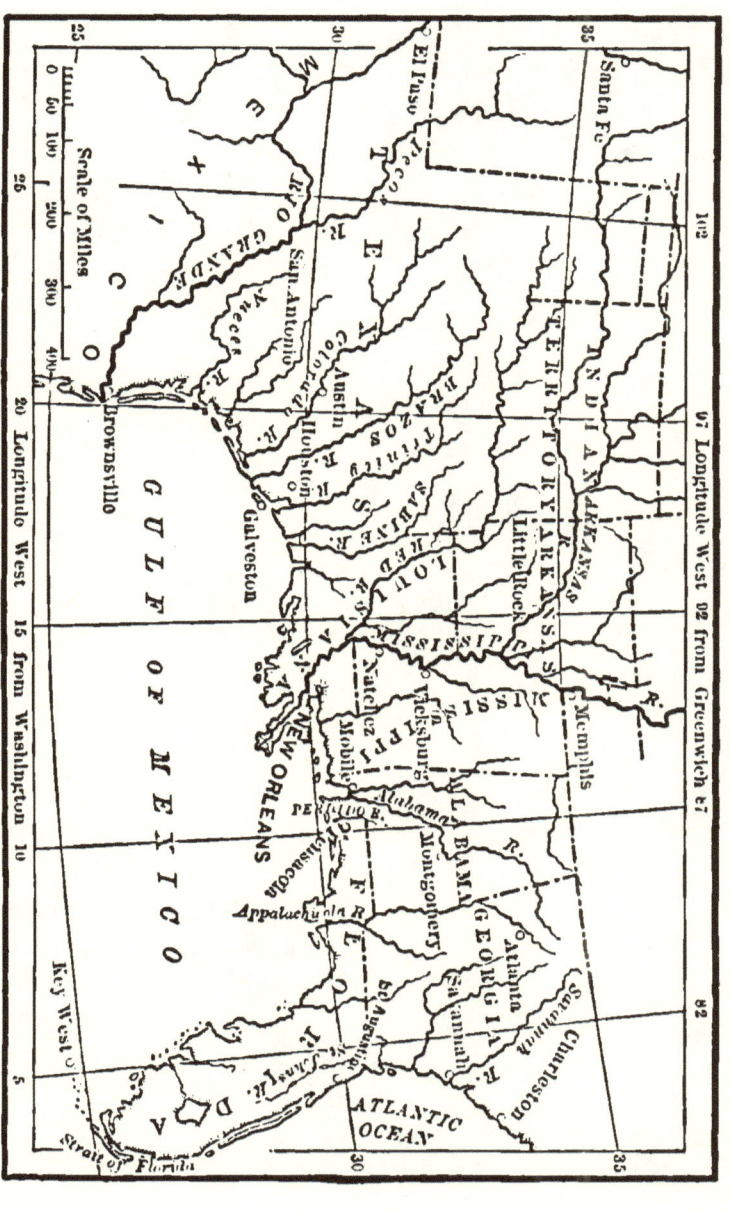

TERRITORY REFERRED TO IN THE NEGOTIATIONS FOR THE ACQUISITION OF FLORIDA.

principles which underlie the mutual rights and duties of independent political communities than the United States. In 1823, Canning, the Prime-minister, distinguished for his thorough knowledge of international law, said in the House of Commons, "If I wished for a guide in a system of neutrality, I should take that laid down by America in the days of the presidency of Washington and the secretaryship of Jefferson." Phillimore, in his great work, says of the Non-intercourse Act of 1809, "It was worthy of the country which has contributed such valuable materials to the edifice of International Law." President J. Q. Adams, in his message, 1826, speaks of our first treaty with Prussia as "memorable in the diplomatic annals of the world, and precious as a monument of the principles in relation to commerce and maritime warfare with which our country entered upon her career as a member of the great family of independent nations." The *Edinburgh Review*, in a notice of Judge Wharton's "Digest," associating him in legal literature with Kent, Story, and Wheaton, recognizes fully the indebtedness of modern international law to the United States, and adds, "The international law of the United States is characterized by a marked individuality and independence of thought. The statesmen of the republic have not felt themselves bound by theories, however venerable, or been troubled by the conflicting views of eminent jurists. They have rested their contentions on clear principles which they have evolved for themselves, and they have enunciated their views without obscurity and with perfect straightforwardness."

The United States had just been admitted as a coequal into the great family, but she was nevertheless regarded as a parvenu, an intruder, and the principles of her Constitution were looked upon with distrust and suspicion, not to say with hatred and contempt, by the crowned heads and those who affirmed and practised the right of coalition against any power that sought to disturb the European equilibrium, or questioned the "right divine" of kings and nobility. At this day, when our power is respected and feared, and our growth and prosperity are an unceasing wonder, we can hardly understand how we were belittled and insulted, and what constant and studied disregard and violation of our equal rights were inflicted in our infancy. A willingness to go to war with France for the maintenance of our dignity, the punishment of the pirates in the Mediterranean, a war with England, extension of territory, an unwavering assertion of our equality, vindicated the right to an independent existence and to a participation in all that belonged to, or grew out of, the intercourse of nations. Perhaps the friction was greater, and the willingness to apply the law which governs external affairs of communities was more reluctant, because of the early avowals of Washington and Jefferson that our cis-Atlantic country was not to be harassed by entangling alliances with European States. Refusing to become an integral part of the great European system, to ally herself with foreign governments in their dynastic wars and endless disputes as to succession, balance of power, and rectification of boundaries, the United States found the European governments inclined to ignore the rights of her citizens and her claim to the freedom of the seas.

Troubles with Spain began during the administration of Washington, and continued up to the slow acknowledgment of the independence of her former colonies, sometimes verging on serious hostilities. As early as 1788, with the connivance and active agency of Gardogue, the Spanish Minister at Washington, an effort was made to detach the trans-Alleghany country from the Union, and in 1792 there was a serious difference of opinion and discussion as to the navigation of the Mississippi. In 1801, Mr. Charles Pinckney, then Minister at Madrid, was instructed to urge on the Spanish Government redress for sufferings from capture by privateers unlawfully cruising out of Spanish ports, and from unlawful condemnations by Spanish tribunals. The spoliations committed on American commerce were so heavy, and tribunals of justice and the Government failing to give redress, a clear intimation was made that more effective measures must be resorted to. The importance of the question, Mr. Pinckney was told, would require all his zeal, patriotism, and delicacy. Some efficient effort was due to the sufferers and "to the dignity of the United States, which must always feel the insults offered to the rights of individual citizens." The irritations with Spain had been aggravated by her possessions on our frontier, by her national pride and sensitiveness, and by her ancient claims of precedence over other States.*

---

* In Evelyn and the Memoirs of Gramont is a curious incident growing out of Spanish arrogance in 1660, at the Court of Great Britain. The Spanish ambassador, on the occasion of the public entry of the Swedish ambassador into London, claimed precedence of the French ambassador. This so offended Louis XIV. that he compelled his rival to submit to the mortification of acknowledging the French superiority.

Appendix D.

The purchase of Louisiana from France, in 1803, excited a controversy between Spain and the United States which continued with more or less acrimony until the whole question of territory and boundary was settled by the acquisition of Florida. The acquisitions of Louisiana and Florida were almost inseparably allied, and our Government, as early as 1804, sought, but in vain, the influence of the French Government in favor of our construction of the treaty, and to help in the acquisition of territory east of the Perdido River. It would be a hopeless task to seek to unravel all the treaties made since that of Utrecht, 1713, which concern the extent and the boundaries of the various territorial divisions between Georgia and the Rio Grande.

In 1763, what was then known as Louisiana was divided between Great Britain and Spain. France lost by this treaty all her possessions in North America. In addition to Canada, she ceded to Great Britain the river and port of Mobile and all her possessions on the left side

---

Louis caused a medal to be struck commemorative of this victory, in which the Spanish ambassador was represented as making the declaration to the king, "No concurrer con los ambassadores de Francia," with this inscription, "Jus præcedendi assertum," and under it, "Hispanorum excusatio coram XXX. legatis principium, 1662."

of the Mississippi, except New Orleans and the island on which it was situated. The residue of Louisiana was ceded to Spain in a separate and secret treaty. The cession of Florida to Great Britain was the price paid for the restoration of Cuba to Spain. Great Britain divided the territory into East and West Florida, and in 1783 ceded them to Spain, and the provinces were known and governed by these names as long as they remained under the dominion of His Catholic Majesty. Spain, thus owning both banks of the Mississippi at its mouth and for some distance above, claimed the exclusive navigation below the point of the southern boundary of the United States. The refusal of the use of the lower river aroused much and indignant feeling in the West. Kentucky and Virginia made vigorous protests against a proposition to concede Spain's right to close navigation. The angry dispute was terminated by the treaty of 1795, one article of which provided that the river should be open to the navigation of the citizens of the United States from its source to the ocean. Another article granted the right of deposit in the port of New Orleans, and to export thence merchandise and effects on the payment of warehouse hire. By the treaty of October 1, 1800, between the French Republic and Spain, known as the St. Ildefonso treaty, Spain made a retrocession to France of the province of Louisiana as at that time possessed by Spain, and "such as it was when France possessed it." When this cession occurred, Great Britain and the United States took alarm. Mr. Jefferson in his message, December 15, 1802, said, "The cession of the Spanish province of Louisiana to France, which took place in the course of the late war, will, if carried into effect, make a change in the aspect of our foreign relations, which will doubtless have just weight in any deliberations of the Legislature connected with that subject." With the sagacity of a statesman he saw how essential the property and sovereignty of the Mississippi and its waters were, to secure an uncontrolled navigation and an independent outlet for the produce of the Western States, "free from collision with other powers and the dangers to our peace from that source," and therefore he authorized propositions to be made for obtaining the sovereignty of New Orleans and of other possessions in that quarter.

The abrupt closing in 1802 of the port of New Orleans, without the assignment of any other equivalent place of deposit, and the injuries sustained until the restoration of the right of deposit, suggested naturally the expediency of guarding against their recurrence by the acquisition of a permanent property near the entrance of the Mississippi into the Gulf. The first propositions were treated by France with decided neglect. "The French Government," said Madison, "had manifested a repugnance to the purchase which left no expectation of an arrangement with France by which an acquisition was to be made, unless in a favorable crisis, of which advantage should be taken." The distress of French finances, the unsettled posture of Europe, the increasing jealousy between Great Britain and France, made "the favorable crisis," and Bonaparte, on April 30, 1803, agreed to sell or cede his new acquisition to the United States. The words of the treaty were somewhat remarkable; but it is important, in view of subsequent discussions and negotiations, to bear in mind that in the transfer the identical language was employed that had been used in 1800, so that the Government of the United States was subrogated, in express terms, to the rights of France and of Spain. Phillimore, in recording this "derivative acquisition" of territory, says, "It belongs to the province of the historian to record the ineffectual regret of deceived and injured Spain, and the sagacity of the United States in profiting by the troubles of Europe, both at this period and subsequently, by the acquisition of Florida."

Spain remonstrated with France against the cession of Louisiana, and endeavored to prevent the execution of the treaty, being not unwilling to use pecuniary arguments if they promised success. Mr. Cevallos, the Spanish Minister for Foreign Affairs, in an interview with Mr. Charles Pinckney, our Minister at Madrid, denied the right of France to make such a cession, alleging that in the preceding cession by Spain to France there was a secret article that France should never part with Louisiana except to Spain, and that if she ever wished to dispose of it, Spain should have the pre-emption.*

---

* American State Papers, 567, 568, 598. The Marquis Casa Irujo, the Spanish Representative, protested against the cession as a sort of crime, and Mr. Onis treated it as a just cause of complaint on the part of Spain. I have applied, through the Minister of Foreign Affairs, for the evidence of this secret agreement, and have been assured that it does not exist in the archives. Besides, the cession by France was made with the full knowledge of Spain, and no objection was made until Irujo's protest. In March, 1803, the American Minister in Spain was informed of the transfer of Louisiana to France, and in answer to an application made by the direction of his Government, Don Pedro Cevallos stated "that by the retrocession made to France of Louisiana that power regained the province with the limits it had, saving the rights

This discontent of Spain increased her unwillingness to make a prompt and peaceable settlement of the vexed questions which had been pending for some years between the two countries, and which every month's delay increased in number and exasperation. In the instructions to Mr. Pinckney, March 31, 1804, Mr. Madison made an elaborate argument to show that the eastern boundary of Louisiana extended to the Perdido. For many years the controversy was waged. The United States insisted that by the treaty of 1800 Spain ceded the disputed territory, as part of Louisiana, to France, and that France, in turn, in 1803, ceded it to the United States. Spain, with equal earnestness and persistence, maintained that her cession to France comprehended what was at that time denominated Louisiana, consisting of the island of New Orleans and the country west of the Mississippi.

---

acquired by other powers; and that the United States could address themselves to the French Government to negotiate the acquisition of territories which might suit their purpose." The Spanish Government was apprised of the intention of the United States to negotiate for the purchase. The Spanish Ambassador witnessed the progress of the negotiation at Paris, and the conclusion of the treaty was promptly known and understood in Madrid. No objection was interposed at the time, and no protest was then made.

C. J. Marshall, in Foster v. Neilson, 6 Peters, 306, said, "Every word in that article of the treaty of St. Ildefonso which ceded Louisiana to France was scanned by the Ministers on both sides with all the critical acumen which talents and zeal could bring into their service. Every argument drawn from collateral circumstances connected with the subject, which could be supposed to elucidate it, was exhausted." Each party adhered to the original opinion and purposes. The arguments, read after fifty years have elapsed, do not, on either side, seem so conclusive as to leave no loop to hang a doubt upon. The very forcible contention of the United States, that France having ceded the province of Louisiana in full sovereignty, with all the rights which belonged to her under the treaty of 1800, the United States succeeded to those rights, was enfeebled somewhat by the declaration of Talleyrand, that by the treaty of St. Ildefonso Spain retroceded no part of the territory east of the Iberville, which had been held and known as West Florida, and that, in all the negotiations between the two Governments, Spain had constantly refused to cede any part of the Floridas, even from the Mississippi to the Mobile. In January, 1805, Mr. Monroe arrived in Madrid, having been commissioned with special authority to act in conjunction with Mr. Pinckney, and he remained over a year in the vain endeavor to effect a settlement of the matters in controversy. Coupled with the adjustment of the Louisiana boundary and other matters in dispute, was a proposition to purchase the whole of Florida for a sum of money which was designedly left indefinite. In the draft of a treaty for the accomplishment of the two principal ends and for the payment of outstanding claims, was a proposition to have, for a term of years, a neutral ground between the west of Louisiana and the Spanish territory, now known as Texas. The neutral territory was to be so limited or defined as not to deprive the United States of the waters flowing into the Gulf between the Mississippi and Colorado rivers.

The voluminous correspondence shows a strong desire on the part of the Government at Washington to terminate amicably all existing differences, and to place the relations between Spain and the United States on a basis of permanent friendship. The extraordinary nature of the commission was a distinct declaration of the critical state of affairs and of the importance of the questions at issue. The United States claimed indemnification for damages done to peaceful and lawful commerce within the jurisdiction of Spain, and for the losses which accrued from the suspension of the right of deposit at New Orleans, as guaranteed by the treaty of 1795. A board of independent and impartial men was suggested, with authority to consider and to adjust counter-claims between the two nations. The gist of the negotiations, however, artful as may have been the attempt not to make too conspicuous, was the settlement of the western boundary of Louisiana and the acquisition of Florida. In the instructions to Mr. Monroe, April 15, 1804, he was (1) to obtain the sanction of Spain to the late cession of Louisiana to the United States; (2) to procure the cession of territory held by Spain east of the Mississippi; and (3) to make provision for the payment of American claims.

The masterly presentation of all the points mooted by our representatives is of interest chiefly to the historical student, because the United States has now undisputed ownership of the whole coast-line from St. Mary's to the Rio Grande, and no question with a foreign power, based on the old contention, can possibly arise. The cases before the Supreme Court,*

---

* 2 Peters, Foster v. Neilson; 6 Peters, Arredondo; 12 Peters, Garcia; 9 Howard, United States v. Reynes; 11 Wallace, United States v. Lynde, etc.

supplemented by the legislation of Congress, have settled the land contests growing out of sovereignty and ownership, which the United States anticipated and tried to prevent. In the progress of the negotiation, Rio Bravo was mentioned as a limit of Spanish and the Colorado as the limit of American settlement. The President was very averse to the occlusion from settlement, for a long period, of a wide space of territory westward of the Mississippi, and to a perpetual relinquishment of any eastward of the Rio Bravo, and the relinquishment, if made, must be conditioned on the entire cession of the Floridas. It was *in arguendo* suggested to Messrs. Monroe and Pinckney that if Spain were engaged in or threatened with war she might be more willing to yield to terms which, however proper in themselves, "might otherwise be rejected by her pride or misapplied jealousy." In an able letter to Cevallos our commissioners said that as the United States surrounded Florida, except where the ocean intervened, it was an object to possess it. The acquisition of Louisiana had minified the importance of the possession, but as long as Spain held it it would be a cause of jealousy and variance, for each nation would be compelled to have a strong force, and other powers would be interested in provoking a rupture. Florida being in the hands of the United States, all cause of inquietude and misunderstanding would be at an end, territories and police would be distinct, military stations would be removed from each other, and neither power would be interested in disturbing the concerns of the other.

On January 28, 1805, the commissioners submitted the project of a convention for the adjustment of claims and the cession of the Floridas. Florida was "known not to be fertile," and no land greed actuated the United States, for they had "territory enough to satisfy their growing population for ages to come." Probably this opinion, that the United States had within their limits what "it will take ages to fill," was caused by the fact, as stated, that "the territory on both sides of the Mississippi is yet a wilderness," and these arrangements, required by mutual interests, were important to be made "while it remained so." These sagacious men had not the vaguest conception of the boundless progress of our people under the energy of free institutions. Reasons of safety and peace were the predominating influence for pressing the acquisitions. The "project" contained what seemed to be a favorite plan in Washington, and which, in the light of subsequent events, seems to us visionary, not to say absurd. "This was the establishment of an intervening neutral territory, to remain such for twenty years, and give time for ulterior arrangements." The submission of the proposed convention led to a prolonged and somewhat acrimonious discussion. At intervals, notes were interchanged. The Spanish Minister of State, Don Pedro Cevallos, by tone, language, utter indisposition to accommodate the business on just principles, annoying and studied delays, became offensive to the commissioners, who, although "hurt" at the treatment they received, exhibited remarkable forbearance and tact. With persistency and iteration, with repeated avowals of respect and desire for peaceful arrangement, and with a commendable abstinence from all recrimination or menace, the contention and wishes of the United States were presented. On the 12th of May, 1805, the commissioners submitted the ultimate conditions on which they were authorized to adjust the points depending between the two Governments, and they are here reproduced with some fulness as illustrative of the points at issue, and the exceeding difficulties of the protracted negotiations which finally added Florida to the Union. "On condition his Catholic Majesty will concede the territory eastward of the Mississippi, and arbitrate the claims of the citizens and subjects of each power, according to the convention of August 11, 1802 (which up to this time Spain had refused to ratify), the convention will agree to make the Colorado the boundary between Louisiana and Spain, establish a district of territory of thirty leagues on each side of the line, which should remain neutral and unsettled forever, and relinquish the claim for spoliations committed by the French within the jurisdiction of Spain and the claim to compensation for injuries received by the suppression of the deposit at New Orleans." The propositions were absolutely rejected, and Mr. Monroe, considering the negotiation concluded, asked and obtained his passports, that he might repair to London, where he was the Resident Minister. Before his departure from Madrid, he and Mr. Pinckney gave an account of their "unwearied and laborious exertions," and of the utter failure of the mission in all its objects.

The recapitulation of the history of the effort to adjust the differences has at this day, when we are quietly enjoying the fruits of this and subsequent negotiations, rather a humorous aspect. Candor, conciliation, urgency, moderation of language, patience, were met by pleas in abatement, pleas for delays, irrelevant discussions, imperious tone, exaggerated pretensions, and a general behavior that made it incumbent on commissioners to argue and protest that they were not the dupes of the management of the Spanish diplomat. Mr. Pinckney soon resigned and returned home. In these hypercritical and iconoclastic days it has become common to disparage that eminent patriot and statesman, James Monroe. An examination of his services in Spain shows exceptional qualifications as a diplomatist: prudence, self-restraint, courtesy, dignity, tact, energy, familiarity with treaties and international law, ability in argument, devotion to his country's honor and interests, marked in a conspicuous manner his public life in this most difficult of all courts. Judge Wharton, more familiar than any other person with our diplomatic history, says in reference to negotiations with England, "that in ability, candor, and fairness, Mr. Monroe's papers stand in the front rank of diplomatic documents."

The Government at Washington, deeply sensible of the importance of the post at Madrid, and of the urgency of the pending questions, appointed James Bowdoin, of Boston, as Minister Plenipotentiary, and afterwards associated General Armstrong in a special mission respecting these delicate Spanish controversies. The object of the United States in reference to the Floridas was clearly made known to them, and equally as explicitly to George W. Erving, who, as secretary of legation, in the absence of his chief, became *chargé d'affaires*. Mr. Erving remained in Spain until August, 1810, when he returned to the United States. From the withdrawal of Monroe and Pinckney to the arrival of Mr. Erving, in July, 1816, as Minister, scarcely anything of a diplomatic character was accomplished between the two countries. The distracted state of Spain, the internal convulsions, and wars with other countries, made it impossible to accomplish anything in the two chief matters intrusted to our representatives. The hostilities between Great Britain and Spain were concluded by the treaty of peace, amity, and alliance of January 14, 1809, when the two belligerents became allies against France, a common enemy, and there ensued that famous Peninsular campaign of Wellington, wherein he out-manœuvred and defeated Napoleon's best marshals, and the more remarkable guerilla contests—a mode of warfare borrowed from the Moors—in which the skill and experience of the best-trained officers and soldiers of France found more than a match in the desultory warfare of the indomitable Spaniards. The prosecution of campaigns required all resources, physical and intellectual. A struggle for dynasty and existence left little leisure or inclination for transatlantic questions. There could have been no more unpropitious period for calm discussion and parting with territory. Besides, Spain was doubly irritated, the United States having been compelled to occupy Florida. This forcible seizure grew out of the claims for spoliations, the inability of Spain to maintain her authority in Florida and repress depredations and insurrections, and the intrusive occupation by Great Britain of Pensacola and other portions of the province. The shifting events in Europe made the passing of Florida into the possession of another power not improbable, and it became imperative to seize and hold the country, subject to future and friendly negotiation.

In 1814, Mr. Anthony Morris, who had authority to receive "informal communications" from the Spanish Government, expressed the opinion that East and West Florida could be purchased. He intimated that ten thousand dollars for douceurs would be "indispensable," as the different departments of the Spanish Government were not sufficiently "regenerated" to allow great hopes of success without the use of means of this description. This suggestion elicited no consideration nor reply. In 1816, January 19, on the renewal of the suspended diplomatic relations, Mr. Monroe, as Secretary of State, suggested to Chevalier de Onis that it furnished a proper occasion for the consideration of the differences in relation to the purchase of Louisiana and the contested limits. In March, 1816, Mr. Monroe informed Mr. Erving that Onis had intimated that the Spanish Government might be willing to cede its claim for territory on the eastern side of the Mississippi in satisfaction of claims, and in exchange for territory on the western side. The United States proposed to accept a cession of Florida as a basis of the release of claims held by citizens of the United States against Spain, and offered at the same time, by way of compromise, to take the Colorado River as the western boundary of the Louisiana purchase, although it had been previously maintained that that purchase extended to the Rio Grande. Mr. Monroe and Mr. J. Q. Adams held very strongly that the Rio Grande was the true south-western boundary. Mr. Onis declared these propositions inadmissible, went into elaborate repetitions of the discussions of 1802–1805, and demanded restoration of places occupied by Federal troops. On July 19, 1818, Don José Pizarro, writing to Mr. Erving, said, "In one of our late conferences I had the honor to state to you anew his Majesty's readiness to cede both of the Floridas to the United States . . . in consideration of a suitable equivalent to be made to his Majesty in a district of territory situated to the westward of the Mississippi." In July and August, Mr. Erving, replying to the Spanish Minister of State, refers to "his Majesty's disposition to cede his possessions to the east of the Mississippi for a reasonable equivalent," and suggests instead of the guarantee of Spanish territory by the United States—a thing which could not be done—a better guarantee in the form of "a desert," or unoccupied, uninhabited tract of thirty leagues on the Colorado, extending up to 32° north latitude, as "a barrier between the possessions" of the two countries. Negotiations between the two countries were suspended, by formal notice, until satisfaction should be made for the proceedings of General Jackson in Florida, which his Catholic Majesty denounced as outrages upon his dignity and honor, and for which he demanded apology and indemnity. John Quincy Adams, in papers which are an enduring monument to his patriotism and ability, "carried the war into Africa," and charged and proved that it was "to the conduct of her own commanding officers that Spain must impute the necessity under which General Jackson found himself of occupying the places of their command." "The horrible combination of robbery, murder, and war with which the frontier of the United States bordering upon Florida has for several years past been visited is ascribable altogether to the total and lamentable failure of Spain to fulfil the fifth article of the treaty of 1795, by which she stipulated to restrain by force her Indians from hostilities against the citizens of the United States." "Had the engagements of Spain been fulfilled, the United States would have had no Seminole War." Far from indemnifying the Crown of Spain for losses sustained, the American Minister at Madrid was instructed that the Crown of Spain should indemnify the United States for the expenses of a war which Spain was bound to prevent.

It is difficult to realize the vexatious vicissitudes which attended this long-drawn-out negotiation. In course of time it at last became apparent, even to Spain, that Florida must come under the sovereignty of the United States. The idea of its transference to another foreign power was not to be tolerated for a moment. Its continued retention by Spain, remote, proud, sensitive, jealous, involved in foreign wars and chronic internal turmoils, would generate ceaseless trouble and necessitate quasi-belligerent forces on the border. Indian incursions and depredations, unprevented by Spanish authorities, made it imperative to cross the line in pursuit, and for the punishment of the savages. "Masterly inactivity," a phrase borrowed by Mr. Calhoun, in his Mexican War speeches, from Sir James Mackintosh, was too feeble a policy. The vigilance of Erving and other Ministers was unceasing. Efforts to purchase were thwarted. Negotiations were begun and suspended. Procrastination was pursued under specific instructions to that end. The patience and forbearance and moderation of the United States had been wonderful. Even Mr. Adams restrained largely his irritability of temper and vitriolism of pen; but this patient submission was manifestly nearing an end. Mr. Onis, seeing that procrastination as a game and a policy was exhausted, sent, on October 24, 1818, to Mr. Adams, a proposition to cede all the property and sovereignty possessed by Spain in and over the Floridas, under certain conditions. The conditions were promptly rejected; a "final offer" on the part of the United States was made; matters grew worse, and belligerent measures seemed imminent. Mr. Adams, October 31, 1818, used this significant language: "The President is deeply penetrated with the conviction that further protracted discussion . . . cannot terminate in a manner satisfactory to our Governments. From your answer to this letter he must conclude whether a final adjustment of all our differences is now to be accomplished, or whether all hope of such a desirable result is, on the part of the United States, to be abandoned." After some letters, showing a wide divergence of views, on January 11, 1819, Mr. Onis announced that by a courier extraordinary from his Government he was authorized to give a greater extent to his proposals. On the 9th he submitted his *projet*, and Mr. Adams on the 13th responded by a counter *projet*. At this point Mr. Hyde de Meuville, the French Minister, at the request of Mr. Onis, "confined by indisposition," had an interview with Mr. Adams, and a full and free discussion of the two *projets*. Explanations and modifications were made, and on February 22, 1819, was signed in Washington "a Treaty of Amity, Settlement, and Limits," which provided for the cession of Florida and "the reciprocal renunciation of certain claims as adjusted by a joint commission." The commissioner had power to decide conclusively upon the amount and validity of claims, but not upon the conflicting rights of parties to the sums awarded by them. Comegys *v.* Vasse, 1 Peters, 193. The spoliation claims held by the United States against Spain were renounced, and the United States undertook to make satisfaction for the same to the amount of five millions of dollars.

The Rio Grande contention was given up, a majority of the Cabinet overruling Mr. Adams, and holding that the immediate acquisition of Florida was too important to be jeoparded, or "clogged by debatable demands for territory to the south-west." The intervening neutral territory, the uninhabited desert, the impassable barrier between the two countries, which for so many years and so often was proposed and relied upon to prevent conflict of jurisdiction and of people, seems to have been quietly ignored. The Louisiana boundary was settled by following the Sabine, Red, and Arkansas rivers as far westward as the 42d degree of north latitude and pursuing that degree to the Pacific Ocean.* In settling disputed boundaries, and,

---

* The conflicting claim of title to territory between Texas and the United States (see President's Proclamation of December 30, 1887) grows out of the terms of this fixing the boundary line between the two countries.

in fact, in making this treaty, the United States did not assent to the claim of sovereignty or ownership over the territory between the Mississippi and the Perdido. Both legislative and executive departments of the Government, prior to 1819, treated territory west of the Perdido as part of the territory acquired from France in 1803, and in Pollard v. Files, the Supreme Court declared as the settled doctrine of the judicial department of the Government that the treaty of 1819 ceded no territory west of the Perdido River.*

The United States exonerated Spain from all demands in the future on account of the claims of her citizens, and undertook to make satisfaction for the same to an amount not exceeding five millions of dollars. It is commonly stated that the United States purchased Florida for that sum of money. In the negotiation the Spanish Minister objected to the article stipulating for the payment, on the ground that it would appear from it that in consideration of that amount Spain had ceded the two Floridas and other territories, when she would not have ceded them for $20,000,000 but for her desire

---

* 2 Howard, 591; Foster v. Neilson, 2 Peters, 253; Garcia v. Lee, 2 Id., 513.

to arrange and terminate all differences with the United States.* In 1805, Monroe and Pinckney, in their proposal to the Spanish Government for the cession of Florida, said that Florida was not valuable for its land, and suggested that the sum paid "for the whole of the province of Louisiana furnished a just and suitable standard" as to what would be proper in paying for Florida. The area of Florida is 56,680 square miles, and Mr. Jefferson paid $15,000,000 for all the country west of the Mississippi not occupied by Spain, as far north as the British territory, and comprising, wholly or in part, the present States of Arkansas, Kansas, Missouri, Iowa, Minnesota, Nebraska, Oregon, and Colorado, and the Indian Territory and the Territories of Dakota, Idaho, Montana, Washington, and Wyoming.

The treaty, submitted to the Senate on the day it was signed, was at once unanimously ratified, thus giving additional lustre to the birthday of Washington. Before the adjournment of Congress, acts were passed authorizing the

---

* In a memoir on the negotiation, published by Onis in 1820, he sought to show that the treaty of cession ought to be considered as a treaty of exchange of Florida for Texas, a country more extensive, fertile, and valuable.

establishing of local governments over the acquired territory. John Forsyth, of Georgia, was appointed Minister to Spain, and he carried with him a copy of the treaty and minute instructions as to the exchange of ratifications.* So confident was the Government of early action, the *Hornet*, which carried Mr. Forsyth, was ordered to remain at Cadiz a sufficient length of time to carry back the ratified copy. So anxious and so certain of speedy assent were the authorities at Washington, instructions were sent to Mr. Erving that it might be expedient for him to exchange the ratifications, if by any accident the formal reception of Forsyth should be delayed "beyond a very few days." Fearing the absence of Mr. Erving, on account of the infirm state of his health, or the non-arrival of Mr. Forsyth, a special messenger, with duplicate copies of treaty and instructions, was sent to Mr. Thomas L. L. Brent, the Secretary of Legation, so that he might exchange the ratifications. After this twenty years of negotiation

---

* Mr. Forsyth was instructed to preserve the right of the United States to the *alternative* of being first named and of the representative to sign first. In the counterpart, the other nation has the like privilege. In 1815, Great Britain claimed as a precedent a previous waiver of this international practice by the United States, but it was withdrawn.

it was supposed that the trouble was ended; but he who measures a Spaniard by the ordinary standard will find himself, in the end, grievously disappointed.

Long experience has been condensed into a popular proverb, *Del dicho al hecho va mucho trecho*—From the saying to the doing is a great distance. The *Hornet* returned in the summer, not with the ratification, but with recriminatory despatches because of the unexpected and inexcusable delay. Spain did not give her assent. She offered various evasive excuses and pretexts. She might promptly have disavowed the treaty as in excess of her instructions. She did not. She consented to the negotiations. She knew what had been done, and seven months passed before she uttered a word of complaint. When it became known that Spain refused to confirm the contract and interposed frivolous excuses for her conduct, much indignation was aroused, and harsh measures had advocacy in the press and in Congress. It was well said the cession was no new thing, and that the agreement, from preliminary steps to final consummation, was as well known in Madrid as in Washington, at least so far as substance was concerned. President Monroe said in his message that Spain had formed a relation be-

Appendix D. 219

tween the two countries which would justify any measures on the part of the United States which a strong sense of injury and a proper regard for the rights and interests of the nation might dictate. Adams contended that Spain was under obligations of honor and good faith; and in a letter to the chairman of the Committee of Foreign Relations, Mr. Lowndes, of South Carolina—author of the phrase, "I had rather be right than be President"—asserted the "perfect right" of the Government to compel a specific performance of the engagement and secure indemnity for the expenses and damages which grew out of the refusal of Spain to ratify. Intemperance of language and proposal was met by wise counsel, and the proposed immediate military occupation was defeated. After weary years of patience and of earnest effort to avoid war, very fortunately the country was not precipitated into it by the hot heads and Hotspurs. It was well determined to await the logic of events, and not hazard the gaining of what must surely, like ripe fruit, fall into our hands. General Jackson once said, "Geography controls my politics," and so the geographical position of Florida made it inevitably a part of the Union. Count Aranda, when he was Prime-minister of Spain, as far back as 1783, distinctly foresaw and acknowledged the necessity of the acquisition.

The irritation felt at the repudiation of a solemn international compact excited general attention, and it was felt that a war might produce grave international complications, and transfer not only Florida but Cuba and Texas also to the United States. France and Great Britain remonstrated with Spain, and she realized that the temporizing and procrastinating policy must give way to positive and definite action. On the 24th of October, 1820, the Cortes having previously authorized and advised, the King, Ferdinand VII., approved and ratified the treaty. Such was the slowness of communication in those days, that four months elapsed before the ratification was known in Washington. (I have received instructions from the State Department by post in eleven days.) The time fixed for joint ratification, six months, having expired, the treaty was resubmitted to the Senate, and ratified a second time, February 19, 1821. On the 22d—again connecting the hallowed day with Florida—the House of Representatives gave their assent to the necessary legislation.

Thus an acquisition long sought for, essential to our internal quiet and to save us from foreign intermeddlings, strifes, and conspiracies, was consummated. For nearly a quarter of a century the negotiations were pursued in Spain or in Washington — sometimes interrupted by fretful suspension of diplomatic intercourse, by the revolutionary disturbances in Spain, by English and French wars, by Spanish tenacity for American possessions, and the incurable propensity not to do to-day what can be deferred until to-morrow. No one can read the correspondence in full without a high appreciation of the patriotism and ability of Madison, Monroe, Pinckney, Adams, and Erving. Their State papers show patience, forbearance, courtesy, dignity, tact, power of argument, familiarity with international jurisprudence, and intense loyalty to our institutions. It is not easy to comprehend the disadvantages under which our able negotiators labored in the earlier periods of our history, when our rights as a member of the family of nations were ignored or grudgingly conceded. The credit of the Florida success is enhanced when we consider the personal and national characteristics of the Spaniards. With unquestioned courage, chivalry, scrupulous observance of etiquette, they are vain, proud, sensitive, distrustful of foreigners, obstinate in their opinions, and possessed of a most patience-wearing disposition to procrastinate. The stoical fatalism of the Moor seems in some of its forms to have been bequeathed to his conqueror.

This protracted negotiation is a noble tribute to American diplomacy. The general public sees the external work, the final result, the actors in the last scene of the historic drama, and is ignorant or unobservant of the quiet secretary or Minister, in his office, at official interviews, in social intercourse, watching for opportunities, seizing propitious occasions, removing prejudices, presenting arguments in every possible aspect, and removing Protean objections. It is he who prepares for the ultimate victory. George W. Erving, far away in Madrid, did more to acquire Florida than every senator who voted to ratify the treaty. It is a pleasant reflection and honoring to our country and civilization that although we were often on the ragged edge of war, yet without a drop of blood the question was settled, boundaries were determined, conflicting claims were adjusted, and a large territory was added to our national domain.

THE END.

THEIR PILGRIMAGE.

By CHARLES DUDLEY WARNER. Richly Illustrated by C. S. REINHART. pp. viii., 364. 8vo, Half Leather, $2 00.

Aside from the delicious story—its wonderful portraitures of character and its dramatic development—the book is precious to all who know anything about the great American watering-places, for it contains incomparable descriptions of those famous resorts and their frequenters. Even without the aid of Mr. Reinhart's brilliant drawings, Mr. Warner conjures up word-pictures of Cape May, Newport, Saratoga, Lake George, Richfield Springs, Niagara, the White Mountains, and all the rest, which strike the eye like photographs, so clear is every outline. But Mr. Reinhart's designs fit into the text so closely that we could not bear to part with a single one of them. "Their Pilgrimage" is destined, for an indefinite succession of summers, to be a ruling favorite with all visitors of the mountains, the beaches, and the spas.—*N. Y. Journal of Commerce.*

The author touches the canvas here and there with lines of color that fix and identify American character. Herein is the real charm for those who like it best, and for this one may anticipate that it will be one of the prominent books of the time. Of the fancy and humor of Mr. Warner, which in witchery of their play and power are quite independent of this or that subject, there is nothing to add. But acknowledgment is due Mr. Reinhart for nearly eighty finely conceived drawings.—*Boston Globe.*

No more entertaining travelling companions for a tour of pleasure resorts could be wished for than those who in Mr. Warner's pages chat and laugh, and skim the cream of all the enjoyment to be found from Mount Washington to the Sulphur Springs.... His pen-pictures of the characters typical of each resort, of the manner of life followed at each, of the humor and absurdities peculiar to Saratoga, or Newport, or Bar Harbor, as the case may be, are as good-natured as they are clever. The satire, when there is any, is of the mildest, and the general tone is that of one glad to look on the brightest side of the cheerful, pleasure-seeking world with which he mingles.... In Mr. Reinhart the author has an assistant who has done with his pencil almost exactly what Mr. Warner has accomplished with his pen.—*Christian Union, N. Y.*

PUBLISHED BY HARPER & BROTHERS, NEW YORK.

☞ *The above work sent by mail, postage prepaid, to any part of the United States or Canada, on receipt of the price.*

BEN-HUR: A TALE OF THE CHRIST.

By LEW. WALLACE. New Edition from New Electrotype Plates. pp. 560. 16mo, Cloth, $1 50; Half Calf, $3 00.

Anything so startling, new, and distinctive as the leading feature of this romance does not often appear in works of fiction. ... Some of Mr. Wallace's writing is remarkable for its pathetic eloquence. The scenes described in the New Testament are re-written with the power and skill of an accomplished master of style.—*N. Y. Times.*

Its real basis is a description of the life of the Jews and Romans at the beginning of the Christian era, and this is both forcible and brilliant. ... We are carried through a surprising variety of scenes; we witness a sea-fight, a chariot-race, the internal economy of a Roman galley, domestic interiors at Antioch, at Jerusalem, and among the tribes of the desert: palaces, prisons, the haunts of dissipated Roman youth, the houses of pious families of Israel. There is plenty of exciting incident; everything is animated, vivid, and glowing.—*N. Y. Tribune.*

From the opening of the volume to the very close the reader's interest will be kept at the highest pitch, and the novel will be pronounced by all one of the greatest novels of the day.—*Boston Post.*

It is full of poetic beauty, as though born of an Eastern sage, and there is sufficient of Oriental customs, geography, nomenclature, etc., to greatly strengthen the semblance.—*Boston Commonwealth.*

"Ben-Hur" is interesting, and its characterization is fine and strong. Meanwhile it evinces careful study of the period in which the scene is laid, and will help those who read it with reasonable attention to realize the nature and conditions of Hebrew life in Jerusalem and Roman life at Antioch at the time of our Saviour's advent.—*Examiner, N. Y.*

It is really Scripture history of Christ's time, clothed gracefully and delicately in the flowing and loose drapery of modern fiction. ... Few late works of fiction excel it in genuine ability and interest.—*N. Y. Graphic.*

One of the most remarkable and delightful books. It is as real and warm as life itself, and as attractive as the grandest and most heroic chapters of history.—*Indianapolis Journal.*

The book is one of unquestionable power, and will be read with unwonted interest by many readers who are weary of the conventional novel and romance.—*Boston Journal.*

PUBLISHED BY HARPER & BROTHERS, NEW YORK.

☞ *The above work sent by mail, postage prepaid, to any part of the United States or Canada, on receipt of the price.*

www.ingramcontent.com/pod-product-compliance
Lightning Source LLC
Chambersburg PA
CBHW021818230426
43669CB00008B/788